I PROMISE YOU

YAEL MERMELSTEIN

I PROMISE YOU

YAEL MERMELSTEIN

Copyright © 2016 Israel Bookshop Publications
ISBN 978-1-60091-473-7

All Rights Reserved

No part of this book may be reproduced in any form
without written permission from the copyright holder.
The rights of the copyright holder will be strictly enforced.

Book design by:

SRULY PERL • 845.694.7186
mechelp@gmail.com

To purchase copies for classroom use, please contact the publisher.

Published and distributed by:

Israel Bookshop Publications

 501 Prospect Street
Lakewood, NJ 08701
Tel: (732) 901-3009
Fax: (732) 901-4012
www.israelbookshoppublications.com
info@israelbookshoppublications.com

Printed in the USA

Distributed in Israel by:	**Distributed in Australia by:**
Shanky's	Gold's Book and Gift Company
Petach Tikva 16	3-13 William Street
Jerusalem	Balaclava 3183
972-2-538-6936	613-9527-8775
Distributed in Europe by:	**Distributed in South Africa by:**
Lehmanns	Kollel Bookshop
Unit E Viking Industrial Park	Northfield Centre
Rolling Mill Road,	17 Northfield Avenue
Jarrow, Tyne & Wear NE32 3DP	Glenhazel 2192
44-191-406-0842	27-11-440-6679

TABLE OF CONTENTS

Acknowledgments..11

PART 1

Pabianice, Poland
September 3, 1939 — Eleven Years Old 13

PART 2

Ghetto Lodz
1940–August 1944..53

PART 3

The Camps
August 1944–May 1945..171

PART 4

Liberation and Beyond
May 1945–December 1946..219

Postscript..273

Dedication

For my dear Safta
Miriam (Maniusia)
Thank you for making every minute of this project so precious.

And in memory of my Saba,
Yehuda Aryeh Leib (Ari Adler) z"l
I still miss you so much.

Yael Mermelstein

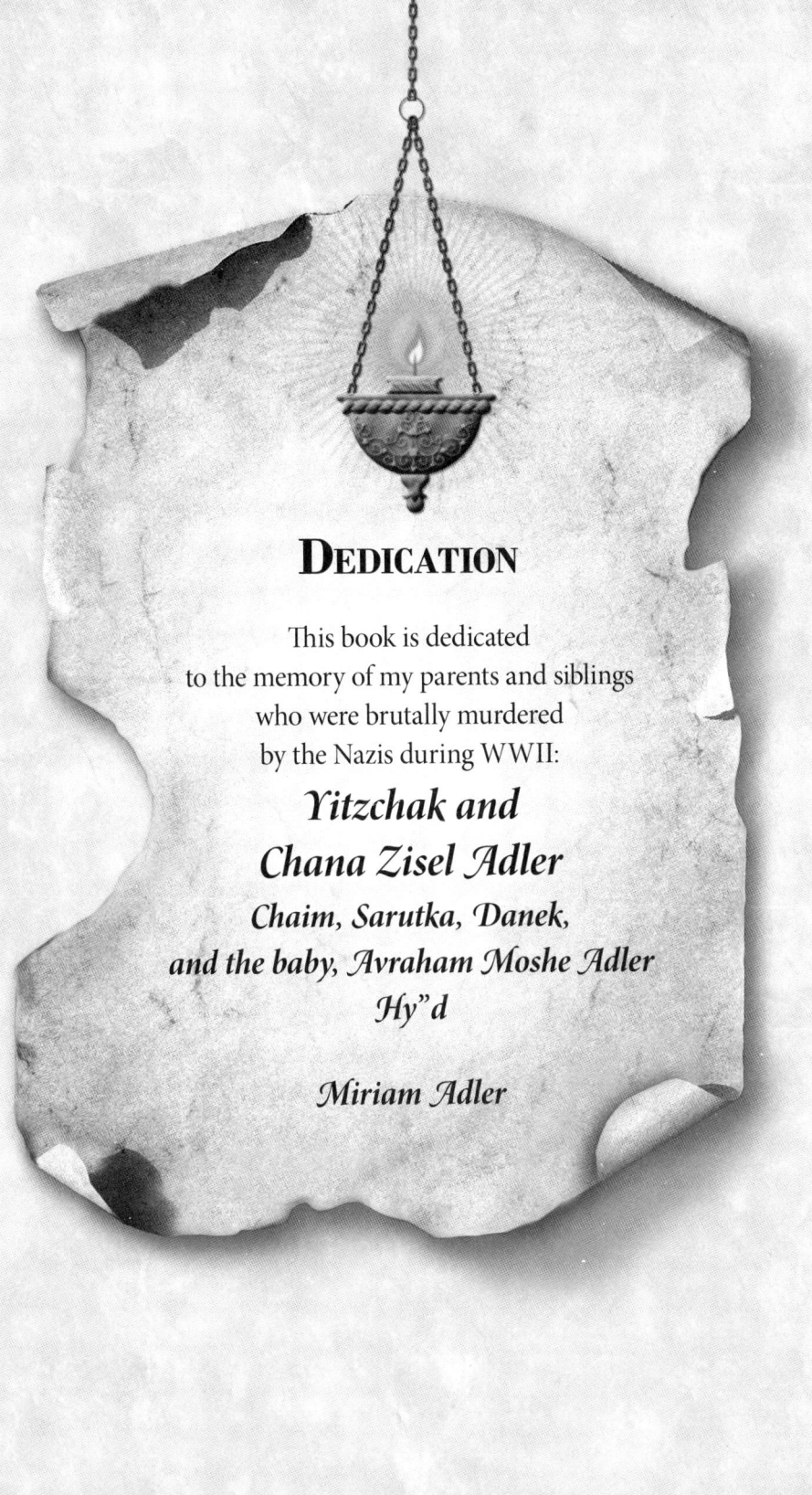

DEDICATION

This book is dedicated
to the memory of my parents and siblings
who were brutally murdered
by the Nazis during WWII:

*Yitzchak and
Chana Zisel Adler*

*Chaim, Sarutka, Danek,
and the baby, Avraham Moshe Adler
Hy"d*

Miriam Adler

Acknowledgments

First and foremost, my thanks to Hashem for allowing me the opportunity to interview my Safta and for giving me the ability to write up her story. I am eternally grateful for this privilege.

Thank you, dear reader, for caring about my Safta's story.

Thank you Tamar Fineberg for being the inspiration behind this whole project.

Thank you Yavneh Academy, Rabbi Burstein, and Dominique Cieri. Your students did a beautiful job. Thank you for honoring my Safta and our family in this way.

Thank you to my wonderful husband and children for everything. A special thank you for letting me spend so much time interviewing Safta and for encouraging me to go to the United States to see the play—an experience I will never forget.

Thank you to my incredible parents, my fabulous sisters, and my amazing in-laws. Thank you to my extended family and to my dear friends who are like family. Thank you Mrs. Salenger. I am so blessed to have such a support system in my life.

Thank you Daddy and Ilana, for providing important feedback that helped me with revisions on this book.

Thank you Mommy and Leora, for helping so much with the interview process, photos, and the myriad back and forth questions.

Thank you to all of my aunts and uncles for being so supportive of this process. I know it was not easy for some of you to watch Safta's story come to life in so many forms. But you also knew it was important to her, and so nothing else mattered to you. You are all wonderful models of *kibbud eim*.

Thank you to all those who insisted this book MUST be published and for never letting me forget it. You know who you are. It really meant a lot.

Safta, how can I adequately thank you and praise you for what you've done here? No part of this was easy for you, no part of it was fun, but you did it anyway. You sat for hours and hours, on Skype and in person, dredging up the prickliest memories. So many times you forced yourself to go on, through tears and both physical and emotional discomfort. You desperately wanted to preserve the memories of your family. You needed their story to be told, and we all needed your story to be told. You did it for us and for them, and every one of us is so incredibly grateful to you. You are an absolute inspiration.

Thank you Israel Bookshop, especially R' Moshe Kaufman and Liron Delmar, for taking a chance on "another Holocaust manuscript." Thank you for recognizing what was special in my Safta's story and for insisting that the world gets to see it, too.

Thank you Malkie Gendelman for your wonderful edits. It was a pleasure working with you.

Thank you Rochelle Gemal and Esther Malky Sonenblick for your impeccable proofreading.

Thank you again to Liron, Malkie, and Esther Malky for your encouragement and for your extreme sensitivity while dealing with this deeply emotional story.

Thank you Sruly Perl of ViviDesign for the magnificent cover. I was all ready to be disappointed. This book is so precious to me there was no way the cover could be good enough. And then it was. Thank you as well for the gorgeous typesetting. For anyone reading this, look at the book and you will understand what I mean.

PART 1

PABIANICE, POLAND

September 3, 1939 — Eleven Years Old

War

In the midst of my early morning dreams

I hear Panna Zuzia's voice,

"Maniusia, wake up!"

Her voice has an edge like cut glass.

I blink.

"Huh?"

"Get dressed," she yells.

"I need to get the little ones."

My elbows sink into the plush mattress beneath me as I try to rise

Slowly.

All my life, I have never been in a rush.

Tata will be in the synagogue praying now,

His tall fur *shtreimel* nodding back and forth, back and forth,

His long satin coat tied at the waist.

Swinging to and fro, to and fro.

I blink at the yellow light streaming through the window.

Even in gray Poland the sun always shines on me.

"Maniusia!"

Yank, yank, goes Panna Zuzia.

Tugging me out from under my goose down comforter.

"Your father is downstairs calling for you. Get dressed. I must get your younger siblings!"

Then, knees swinging over the bed,

The hem of my nightgown dusting the floor.

Panna Zuzia crouching down.

Looking into my eyes.

"There is a war," she says.

Cocoons

What do I know from war?

War is something for other eleven-year-old girls.

Girls who live in countries whose names appear in books,

Girls who know a thing or two about a thing or two.

Two weeks ago I bumped into my cousin, Rita Klainplacz,

At the market in Pabianice.

"War, war, war," Rita said as the adults jabbered.

"It's all the adults ever talk about. What is it anyhow?"

"I don't know," I said. "But let it come and be done with already!"

My parents spin me a cocoon,

I lie nestled inside of it,

Not hearing. Not seeing. Not thinking.

And now, I can smell Panna Zuzia's fear,

Like burnt bread.

The First Time We Run

I throw open the door to my wardrobe,

Painted white as my nightgown,

Legs thick as an elephant's.

Outside, sirens moan like babies,

But I choose a frock, anyway,

Pink gingham with a row of fasteners soldiering down the front,

And Panna Zuzia buttons it for me.

We meet Mama in the hallway,

One of her slender arms clutching my baby brother Fishel Dan—Danek—to her chest,

The other hand clenched by my brother Chaim.

Mama has not been well lately,

And I'm afraid she will topple over.

"Sarah!" Panna Zuzia's voice sounds

Like she's swallowed gravel,

And she is spitting it back up.

My sister Sarah races into her open arms.

We sprint down the stairs,

Doors opening all around us,

Our building a gap-toothed smile.

Three floors to the bottom,

To the first floor,

Pabianice, Poland

Where the Baruch family lives.

Rush, rush, rush.

Feet clomping,

Running,

Stomping.

Outside the siren is loud as

A baby wailing in your ear—wishing, wishing

It would just stop.

You know how sometimes on a still night,

You can hear your heart beating inside your chest?

Amid all this noise I can hear it even now…

Th-th-thump, th-th-thump, until,

I see Tata which slows my heart to…

Thump, thump, thump

Because seeing Tata feels like finding

The last piece of sky

In a thousand-piece puzzle and

Nothing terrible can happen if

Tata is here.

Waiting

We run with Tata

Stumbling,

Tripping,

Running,

Frantic.

Tata sings a prayer,

I lift my eyes up to the heavens,

His voice like the finest violin,

The same voice that wakes me each morning as he learns the holy Torah.

"All is *gut*, Maniusia," he tells me.

"The *Eibishter*, G-d, is good."

His fingers pressing against my forehead and—

My hand,

Resting on top of Danek's soft curls.

It isn't long before another siren sounds.

"That means all-clear," Tata says.

All clear?

But I have never been more confused.

About Me

Allow me to share a bit about myself,

Or you will not know who it is that runs down the stairs,

Her heart gobbling up her throat.

I am Maniusia Adler,

Born after two babies birthed at home who

Never took a breath.

Thankfully Mama birthed me in a hospital,

And I breathed plenty from the beginning,

Wailing and punching the air,

Like I had a bone to pick with it.

Mama is called Chana Zisel.

Tata is Yitzchak,

Important names for respected chassidim of the Rebbe of Gur.

Me they called Maniusia,

Pronounced *Ma-nyoo-sha*,

The Polish version of Miriam,

Sister to Moshe Rabbeinu, Moses,

A righteous woman

Who played a mean tambourine and

Pulled the entire Jewish nation to sing.

They brought me home to our apartment in Pabianice,

Where we had one of the only telephones in the whole city.

I suppose from the moment that I arrived,

I was connected to something bigger—

Than just me.

Warszawska Street

We don't just own our apartment,

We own the whole building!

One apartment for my *bubbe* and *zeide*,

Another for the Grand Rabbi of Pabianice,

And a *beis medrash*—a special place for learning the holy Torah.

(Tata doesn't just own our building.

He also owns a textile factory, and

I wouldn't blink if you'd tell me

That Tata owns the entire world.)

Two of my *chochas* live here too,

My father's sister and my mother's.

The whole of Warszawska Street,

Is like a pomegranate bursting with Adler seeds.

Warszawska Street 37

If you are to know me,

I must tell you about the inside of my apartment.

My feet pad on

Parquet floors.

My fingers leave prints behind to tell my stories,

Our furniture is heavy as a tram,

Made by Koz'uch—"Who doesn't know their furniture?"

That's what Mama says.

I have a room of my own,

And across the hall sleeps our governess,

Panna Zuzia.

If I want to summon her,

I ring the bell in my room,

Which connects to a central board,

In the kitchen.

Water gurgles under the floor,

And an indoor lavatory! That doesn't leave you

Defrosting your toes near the hearth,

During the frigid winters,

Not that we would need a fire to keep warm

Since we have central heating.

My home is a castle compared to that of my friends.

Ruta lives with three siblings in one room.

If my body were a house,

That room is a tight fist.

With a kitchen, but no water,

And a toilet shack downstairs,

With its back to the wind.

Bala and her family live in three rooms

Like railroad cars;

You walk through one to get to another.

And Henya lives in a room behind the fish store.

You pinch your nose before you walk in.

It is no wonder that all of my friends

Come to play by me.

But I am not left to my own devices! Oh no.

Tata is a very important man, but,

Even though his factory runs him like a clock,

And he spends his empty hours studying the holy Torah,

There is always room for:

Me,

Chaim,

Sarah,

And Danek.

And because of:

Panna Zuzia the governess.

Hela the governess's helper.

Bronia the cook.

And Nadja the cleaner.

There is enough of Mama to go around, too.

Because few in Poland can even dream of all that we have,

Mama says we should count our blessings.

Show gratitude to the One above.

But how can you be grateful

For something you tumble into

The moment you enter the world?
Like being thankful for your nose
Or the ten fingers wagging on your hands.
Impossible!

Not Like It Matters

My parquet floors and my wide bellied dressers,
Don't help to make me any less scared,
When the Nazi soldiers invade Pabianice.
I am only eleven years old,
Used to having my hair combed for me,
And unused to the slightest disturbance.
As if the air raid sirens weren't enough?
Now I stand on my *bubbe's* balcony and I watch—
I watch Nazi soldiers—coming, coming, and even more coming.
Droves and droves of them descending on my Pabianice
Like flies to rotting fruit.
Marching,
With the legs of a centipede,
Their uniforms without a wrinkle, their backs without a wrinkle,
Guns pointed straight at the sun.
I have never seen a gun before today.
I don't even know what a gun can do.
Soon enough, I will learn.

Walking to the Moon

"We are leaving."

That is what Tata says to Mama, standing next to the table in the dining room,

The one with the secret compartment where Mama stows

Her Psalms and her French books.

In the foyer, I cover one ear, the ear that doesn't want to hear what comes next.

With the other ear, I listen.

"Everyone is leaving," he says. "You've heard what they did on the way from Wielun?"

He speaks a question but his voice sounds like a row of exclamation points.

"Where will we go?" Mama asks. "The soldiers have taken over the tramways, the trains…"

"We'll walk to Warsaw but first we will stop in Lodz," Tata says.

I hear my own gasp with my uncovered ear.

Walk to Lodz?

Lodz where Bubbe and Zeide live? Far, far away Lodz?

It is like asking our weak Mama to walk to the moon.

Tata sighs.

It is a sigh that sounds like it has gathered so many things,

Before finally becoming a sigh.

"Get the children. Grab some things.

They say the Germans will never reach Warsaw."

Pabianice, Poland

Exodus

Mama comes,

Holding on to the lintel of my room,

Unsteady on her feet,

"We must leave, *mamele*."

I nod. I already know.

Too soon, we are downstairs.

The street looks like

G-d has spilled a country full of people on it.

Men packing,

Women holding fat babies,

And everywhere people walking in circles like

They don't want to finish,

What has been started.

Tata has fashioned a baby carrier out of a suitcase.

He hoists it on his back and he crouches down.

"Come, Danek," he calls to my brother. "A piggyback ride."

Danek climbs inside.

Mama holds Chaim's hand.

Sarah and I have each other.

We walk and walk

and walk and walk,

The crowd humming around us.

Everyone, walking—

Pook, pook, pook.

The sounds of a million shoes on the pavement,

The sounds of feet pointed toward Warsaw,

Leaving.

Not Far Enough

Tata sings softly.

Sarah's ankles begin to sag inward.

"Are you okay?" I ask her.

She nods, her mouth twisted in pain.

I feel the blisters blooming on my feet.

Fishel Dan wraps his hands around Tata's eyes, playing peek-a-boo.

There is an odor in the air of

Rank bodies, sweat, tears and something else I can't place.

But—

Mama, who's been feeling so unwell lately,

Look how she walks so straight!

And Tata is here with his shoulders broad enough for

The world to perch upon.

I don't know who decides it is time to rest,

But as our steps begin to wobble,

The entire sea of people sit,

Like a wheat field bent by a sudden gust of wind.

I rub the soles of Sarah's feet,

Not minding the stink of her toes,

Just wanting to take some of her ache away.

I hear the planes before Mama and Tata do.

I look up into a bright ball of sun.

Everyone around me looks up too,

A million hands shielding a million pairs of eyes.

The planes dip low, buzzing like oversized bees,

Lower, lower, lower,

Till I can nearly make out the faces of the pilots.

Tok-tok-tok.

What is that noise?

I feel Tata pushing me.

"Maniusia, lie here," he yells.

We lie on the floor in a row—

Mama and Chaim like one bundle,

Then me holding Sarah,

And Danek in his carrier.

Tata stands over us all.

I lie there, nestled in his shadow.

Tok-tok-tok.

People scream.

They run this way and that way

Like scattered marbles,

The screaming grows louder.

"Mama! What's happening?"

"Shhhhhh!"

Then yelling.

"They're shooting at us! They're shooting at us!

Gut in Himmel, they're shooting at us!"

Tata's shadow moves and I can see the planes.

Tok-tok-tok.

I close my eyes.

Open them.

I look at Tata and that's when I see—

His eyes closed,

Lips moving in prayer.

Arms spread as far as they can reach,

His body trying to protect his family.

But they can't reach far enough—

To cover us all.

About My Tata

If someone could stretch his arms,

Doubling or even tripling them in length,

It would be my *tata*.

He is a chassid,

Which means so much more than just,

Twisty sidelocks.

A chassid is knee-deep in

Fear of the Lord.

And my *tata*—

From the tip of the fur *shtreimel* on his head—

To the *gartel* tied round his waist—

To the hem of his *bekeshe*—

The whole length of him shines with fear of the Lord.

Each morning I wake to the sound of him learning the holy Torah

When the sun is just a shadow

And the moon, still whispering goodbye

He and his study partners—

Shmiel Hirsch Kravicki, Itche Meir Yoskowicz, and Leibel Reiss.

All right-hand men of the Rebbe of Gur, everything about them looking so important,

Their thumbs jab at the air to make a point.

The hairs of their beards tickle the pages of the Talmud they study.

They always learn by us because Tata has a *gabinet*, a room just for learning.

Oh, what a glorious alarm clock—

Are these sounds of Torah,

Better than the cockiest rooster.

Tata's Torah is part of the reason that

When he goes to Gur to visit the Rebbe,

People dozens of years older than him stand in respect for him!

Oh! Tata! He is a pot boiling over with wisdom!

If the Rebbe is second to G-d, then Tata must be third!

He will know his way out of this strangeness.

He most certainly will?

Lodz

After such a journey,

Dodging bullets

(Mama says I have dodged nothing worse than a cold during my eleven years),

Our weary bodies reach Lodz,

And I feel my soul is just as weary.

Bubbe and Zeide find us an apartment to stay in,

Bubbe's cousin, Shia Leszczynski,

Who already ran ahead to Warsaw,

Left us his empty nest.

We are like ants,

When the Germans smooth over our hill,

We poke our heads out,

From another mound.

Shelter

The same sirens that wailed in Pabianice,

Cry in Lodz too.

At least in Lodz there are

Shelters.

The cellar in our building

Is dark and clammy.

Tata still sings,

Like honey spilling in this dank place.

Chaim leans his head on Tata's shoulder.

Mama holds Danek and Sarah on her lap.

Mama is tired, more tired every day.

I try not to think of what might be wrong.

I dab at her forehead with a handkerchief in the steamy cellar.

Woomp!

Everything goes dark.

I try to breathe but I can't suck in any air.

I try yelling for help but no voice comes out.

All of these days in the cellar and now finally a bomb has fallen.

Perhaps I am already dead.

Then suddenly, I hear Tata yelling.

"Get off of her! Off!"

Something lifts.

I can see and breathe and I become undead,

All at once.

Tata glowers at a man.

"What kind of a thing is that?

To fall asleep on top of an eleven-year-old girl? You nearly crushed her!"

The man is old,

Maybe forty years,

With gray threads in his beard,

Eyes as big as peach pits,

And piano fingers.

"Forgive me," he says.

"I've been walking three days straight.

Not one blink of an eye of sleep.

I don't even know where I'm finding the strength to—

Speak right now,

And I cannot stay upright a moment more."

Tata's features relax.

He touches a finger to the man's shoulder and then

Scrunches over closer to us,

Giving this man more space to rest his weary frame.

The look on that man's face!

I will never forget it.

Like he's been handed a featherbed instead of

An extra sliver of concrete.

Some Go Home

Tata says,

"Things in Lodz are

No better than in Pabianice,"

After we'd been here only three days.

"The Germans won't be stopped at Warsaw," he says.

"They want to gobble up the entire country,

And the Poles are corrupt enough

To let them do it."

I want to go home.

I miss my bed.

I miss our cook, Bronia, and

The smells of fish and chicken soup

In the kitchen.

Even though I know that:

Panna Zuzia,

Bronia,

And all the others,

Are running for their lives somewhere else,

I can't help but miss it all.

But.

I hear my parents' whispers.

I put together the puzzle in my head,

Because nobody tells me otherwise.

Nobody ever tells me otherwise.

The Nazis are looking for seven prominent men from Pabianice.

When they find them—they will—

I cannot say the rest.

One of those men is—

Tata.

Tata bends down and takes my small hand in his big one.

"I will stay here in Lodz, Maniusia," he says.

"Here, I will stay safe for you.

They will come looking for me—the Germans.

Never tell them where I am.

Never tell your younger siblings where I am.

They won't be able to hold it inside,

The way that you can."

I cling to his shoulders.

I want to kick and scream,

But I am holding too much inside,

There is no room left for screams.

We leave without Tata and

I feel like I need to hold up the sky,

The world is that heavy.

In Charge

Back in Pabianice,

Mama is still unwell and

I am in charge of my siblings.

I, who have never been in charge of anything,

Even of dressing myself.

What do I know?

I know nine-year-old Chaim.

Oh, Chaim!

The morning after Chaim was born,

I walked into the living room,

Still rubbing the sleep from my eyes.

In the middle of the room, there was a mountain,

A hill of new toys.

Mama stood beside it, holding a squirmy bundle.

"What is this?" I asked.

"You have a new brother," Mama said.

"And he brought you toys," Tata said.

And so I loved Chaim right away,

Chaim, giver of gifts.

I know my sister Sarah,

Sweet as an angel.

I thought that when Sarah was born,

Our family was a fresh sheet of factory cotton,

Without any holes.

But there was one hole still waiting to be plugged.

When we came home from the spa at Rabka one summer,

We had a wonderful surprise,

My brother Danek had been born!

Oh, that shimmering hair!

His sweet, twitchy nose.

I didn't need toys from Baby Danek,

In order to love him.

I might not know much about being in charge,

But I know that I love,

My three charges.

Is This Home?

For two months,

We are home.

I try to tend to Mama as best I can.

Our cellar is stocked with potatoes and coal,

But we finish the potatoes fast,

And we can't eat the coal,

Much as we want to.

If we stand on line all night we can collect

Pabianice, Poland

Our food rations,

Special for the Jews,

But we have no Tata

And Mama is too ill to stand.

"What shall I eat, Maniusia?" Sarah asks me,

Rubbing her stomach.

Danek cries.

I take water and

Sand from the street and I

Mix it into an unpalatable cake.

I have never been hungry before.

I don't know the ways of the hungry.

One night, Tata's brother Feter Yankel knocks on our door,

His arms bulging with bread—for us.

The children jump on it.

It tastes like manna from heaven.

"I will wait on line for you," he says. "You won't be hungry anymore."

Feter Yankel waits hours on line to feed his wife and child.

Then he waits again, hours, pressing on his tired, tired feet,

To feed—us.

Old Me, New Me

We are still hungry,

But not hungry enough to care.

I don't know when

My purpose in life changes from

"Thrive" to "survive."

I think I dropped my old self somewhere

On the road between Lodz and Pabianice

And stepped on it with my

Blistered feet,

Until the ground simply

Swallowed "old me" up.

Now I worry all day

About Tata in Lodz,

About Mama moaning in her bed,

About Sarah and Chaim and little Danek.

I have no worry left over for me.

Keeper of Secrets

One morning there is a frantic banging at the door.

Mama jumps from her bed,

Her nightgown rising like a hot air balloon behind her.

I haven't seen her move this fast

In months.

She stops, looks at me, puts a finger to her lips.

I will need to make my words invisible.

The German soldiers shout,

Barging in—

Big and bulky,

Thick batons at their waists—

Their boots scuffing our beautiful floors.

In their outstretched arms,

Revolvers black as night.

I understand their German as

I have a passion for language and

Mama had taught me German,

A blessing turned suddenly to a curse.

"Where is he?" they shout.

Mama holds me close.

"I don't know."

Her voice is stronger than

Our beaten down front door.

A soldier bends down.

He looks me in the eye.

His breath smells

Like the breath of a dog.

"Where is your papa?" he asks me.

Almost kindly.

Like he wants to take me for a stroll

In the park,

His revolver dangling like

A picnic basket between us.

I muster up a brick of courage,

Squeeze it through my lips.

"I wish I knew. I miss my *tata*. But I don't know where he is."

I am an eleven-year-old keeper of secrets.

I am a hundred-year-old keeper of secrets.

They leave.

Mama and I slide to the floor, holding each other, holding ourselves,

Breathing, breathing, breathing.

"They'll be back again," Mama says.

I know they will.

Monsters never visit only once.

All in One Day

The tramways to Lodz are running and

Mama says I can go see Tata!

She doesn't need to tell me twice.

I urge the tram to go faster, faster,

Not that it listens to me.

When I come to Lodz,

Pabianice, Poland

It is nearly time to turn around.

But when I see Tata,

When he scoops me into his neck,

And he smells like his holy books,

When I step back and stare at him,

When he says, "My darling daughter!"

It is like looking at the sunshine.

And it doesn't matter one bit,

That the moment my foot hits the ground in Lodz,

I already have one foot back in Pabianice.

What's Growing in Mama

All that worry over Mama,

I look at her now and I understand

Mama is unwell because,

She is growing a baby.

That's what all the fuss was about.

A baby!

Rosh Hashanah

I startle as I wake up,

Seeing Mama

Holding on to the doorpost,

Her face the color of potatoes,

But perhaps everything

Reminds me of potatoes now.

I sit up quickly.

I do everything in a hurry now.

"What, Mama?"

"It's Rosh Hashanah," she says.

I tremble to think of all I have to pray for

On this holy day of the year.

The prayers beat in my chest,

Like a flock of birds.

"There's something going on," Mama says.

"The men say there are soldiers downstairs.

There are rumors.

They won't hurt a child.

Go down and check, Maniusia."

I pull on something, anything to wear.

Run down the stairs

Across the street

To the synagogue, our shul.

Soldiers stand by every entrance.

Hands clenched round their guns

The way one holds

An important package.

I know who is inside that synagogue.

Too many people that I love.

I run to the back window,

Wheezing short little breaths.

"There are soldiers!" I shout through the small window.

"Dozens of them. Run, run!"

They run.

Dressed in long white *kittels*,

Faces like scared angels.

The soldiers grab them by their beards,

Cutting and tearing them off as they drag them—

To trenches

Dug nearby

To protect against bombings,

Filled with water from

Recent rains.

They force the men to their knees.

I see my uncle, Feter Yankel.

My grandfather, Zeide Adler.

I look right.

Left.

Down.

Up to G-d in Heaven.

Please.

Someone.

Anybody.

Nobody.

A soldier takes my grandfather's head.

Pushes it under the water.

The water gurgles,

Small bubbles.

His body thrashes like

A caught fish.

They push his head deeper.

Deeper.

Deeper.

Then, just before he is gone

Forever

They pull him out.

He gasps for breath,

His mouth opening and closing,

Before the soldier shoves his head

Back under again

And again.

And I feel everything good

Sliding out of me

As my grandfather—

My precious *zeide*!

My uncle,

Feter Yankel!

And all the others

Are nearly drowned

And left on the ground,

Flailing like beached fish,

Half dead,

And maybe wishing

The Germans had finished the job

So they wouldn't have to go on living

In a world that looks

Like this one.

About My *Zeides*

You cannot know what it is to watch your *zeide*,

In such a situation,

But you do not even know my *zeides*.

I will tell you about them.

Zeide Blass, Mama's father, lives in Lodz.

He stands over six feet tall.

The Jewish giant of Lodz.

When I ask him questions he says,

"I'll tell you when you're a big boy."

"I'm not a boy!" I say and

He squeezes my cheek,

Leaving a two-fingered mark behind.

At night he makes sure that

He says *Hamapil* with me first—

The night prayer asking G-d's holy angels,

To watch over you while you sleep.

After *Hamapil,*

You're not allowed to talk

Until morning,

And Zeide Blass wants to stop my chatter,

If only for a few hours.

My tongue burns in my mouth

But I never speak.

Until.

One time he tells me that I'm allowed to speak if it's an emergency.

From then on, *everything* becomes an emergency.

And Zeide Adler!

Zeide Adler is older than Zeide Blass.

Zeide Blass is still busy with business but
Zeide Adler is busy helping.
He started an old age home and he
Has clothing, food, and shelter
For everyone.
Zeide Adler always has a cigarette hanging
From the corner of his mouth,
Which his wife can't stand.
"Chaya Golda," he asks her.
"Maybe you want one, too?"

November 1939

Evacuate!

The Nazis say that
They will evacuate our block
In Pabianice.
I want to stay at home
Even if home means grumbling tummies,
It is still mine.
Mama is too ill to pack,
A wrung washcloth pressed to her eyebrows,
And so my shoulders stoop a little lower,

From this new burden that I carry.

I find two trunks,

And sift through our belongings,

Every frock, every pair of socks and some pictures,

Deciding which of our treasures,

We can do without.

In the end, I stuff them full of clothing and bedding,

They should just be brimming,

Squeeze the air out of each corner,

To make room for more.

But when Feter Yankel comes to pick us up,

To take us to his home at Konstantynowska 3,

An address that is still untouched by

Evacuation!

The Germans are yelling from the street—

"*Raus! Raus!*"

I am rushing so hard that

I call to my uncle on the street.

"Feter Yankel! Catch!"

And I begin tossing our things from the window.

That day in Pabianice,

Luggage rains from the sky

Like bullets.

Still in Pabianice

In Feter Yankel's apartment,

Me.

Mama.

Chaim.

Sarah.

Danek.

Feter Yankel.

Zeide Adler.

Bubbe Adler.

And four others.

Every day taking up more space,

Like bread rising.

Our beautiful apartment,

With the indoor lavatory,

Cordoned off,

Taken over,

Gone.

And nobody even paid Mama a *grosz* for it.

"We may as well go to Lodz," Mama says.

"Maybe there things will be better than here."

Joy fills my body,

The spaces between my bones,

The blood that runs through me like a river,

I inhale it through my nose,

Tata!!!

PART 2

GHETTO LODZ

1940–August 1944

Reunited

Seeing Tata again is like

The feeling you have

When you wake up in the morning,

And something tickles your brain,

But you can't remember what it is.

Until.

You hear shuffling outside your door,

Whispering,

Shhhhhhhhhhhhhhhhhhhhh.

A smile pastes itself on your sleepy face,

Because you've remembered.

It's your birthday!

Smooth

But I barely recognize,

My *tata*,

Without his beard.

The Germans tore Tata's beard from his face,

Like it was a Purim costume.

His cheeks are smooth against mine.

If a beard could speak, I think Tata's would say,

"Yitzchak Adler and I belonged together.

I made him regal!

I made him fine!

I was so much more than just a beard."

The Germans do not allow the men to wear beards,

Or Jewish hats.

One cannot tell a Jewish scholar,

From a street-sweeper.

"*That*," Tata says,

"*Is exactly their point.*"

Hungry 1

I thought that what we'd felt in Pabianice,

Stomachs growling like fierce lions,

Every dream with food as

Its main character:

Chaim Cholent

Naomi Noodle

Pinchos Potato,

That was hungry.

But this new hungry,

Should have its own name,

This banging in your bones hungry,

This scooping out your soul hungry,

This munching on your mind hungry.

This kind of hungry.

My brother Danek cries all day,

"Mama, please can I have something to eat?"

"But I have nothing," Mama says.

"I have nothing."

"Well, then, can I please have bread with nothing?" he asks.

But even that, she cannot give.

Egyptian Mummies

We try playing a game with Danek,

To help him forget about

Hungry

For a bit.

He stands near the fireplace,

In my grandparents' house.

Above it is a mirror,

Reflecting his sweet face.

"Now say, *Egypskia Mumia*," Mama tells him.

"Babibska bubia,"

He watches his lips move in the mirror.

His laugh is like a song.

"Egypskia Mumia," I say.

"Tatiska Tuma."

We laugh,

So happy that,

His mouth is full,

Even if it is only with consonants,

Instead of grapes.

"Egypskia Mumia," we say.

"Egypsa Muma."

We clap so hard our fingers nearly fall from our hands.

We clap so hard they must hear us all the way in America.

I Remember Hungry

I remember, long ago, I remember hungry!

Of course it was not me who was hungry then.

It was at Chaim's *bris milah.*

I wore a dress to his circumcision, which took place in our house,

Navy blue with a pink bow soft as my skin.

The rabbi sat at the head of the table,

Fur *shtreimel* gleaming, *bekeshe* black as a moonless sky.

In the corner of the room, a beggar sat,

His clothing tattered and torn,

Sitting on his hands, waiting for something to eat.

The food arrived!

Golden chicken thighs, crusty potato kugel, bright purple beet salad.

They served the gleaming, glowing rabbi first.

I ran to Mama and I cried—

"The beggar is hungry. The rabbi is full. Why did you give the rabbi first?"

Mama looked at Tata with eyes full of conversation,

And so they gave the beggar second,

But I would always remember that he should have gotten first.

I suppose now, I am the beggar.

Russia

I hear Tata telling Mama

That he wants to take us all to Russia.

Out of this hungry.

Out of this place where there isn't even,

Bread with nothing.

I love my Pabianice

But my Pabianice wears a mask now

And I can't recognize it,

Not even its tiny bits.

And this Lodz,

With its new kind of hungry,

Is like a monster with claws,

Coming closer,

With stretched out arms.

Russia sounds far.

But Russia—

Perhaps in Russia there are sugar cubes

To sip tea through and

Yellow bananas like boats filled

With fleshy deliciousness and

Soft prunes that,

Dot your fingers and

The space above your lip,

With sticky goo.

I would like to visit that Russia.

But then Tata says that his parents, our *bubbe* and *zeide*,

Cannot come.

They are too old.

Too tired.

Poland had already settled in their bones.

And you can't yank it out of them.

I suppose that's what happens,

When you live long enough in one place,

And Tata, dear Tata, what did he say next?

"I won't leave my parents behind.

They need me."

Sweet Mama,

Her body is frail

From growing a person in it,

And from this hungry,

But her mind is like a crusty loaf of bread

Crisp and hard.

"Then we won't leave them," she says.

"Because they need you.

And who knows if things would be better

Somewhere else.

In the merit of fulfilling the commandment

Of honoring your parents,

Surely we will only be blessed."

I feel like someone has sucked the air out of me

And given it to someone else.

Someone else who is going to

Russia.

The Happiest *Yahrtzeit*

Some neighbors in my *zeide's* building,

The Tolniks,

Have managed to hang on to

Some money

From before the war.

They make a meal in honor of

 A rebbe's *yahrtzeit*,

The day their esteemed rabbi died,

So many years ago.

Only men are invited,

Tata among them.

"You will come with me," Tata tells me.

"You will eat until your belly is swollen and plump."

At the meal, Tata tucks away a roll for me.

"Eat, Maniusia," he says.

I think of what my favorite cousin, Leibel, would say.

Take advantage!

The roll is the color of the

Wheat it was ground from,

Sprinkled with

A few drops of sunshine,

And a smattering of poppy seeds,

Small as pinpricks.

I lift each seed,

With the back of my thumb,

Run it across my tongue,

Suck it like a lozenge,

Then swallow,

Pretending each one,

Is a leg of chicken,

A potato flan,

The lightest *wieczorowka*.

And then the roll itself,

Buttery, even without butter,

Soft as a cloud.

I roll pieces big as peas,

Then chew it once on each tooth,

So that none will feel left out,

Swish it around the insides of my cheeks,

Like a wash for my mouth,

Then swallow it,

Sad to see it go,

But knowing it is going

To a better place.

I can't help being happy,

About this *yahrtzeit*.

Even though a big tzaddik, a righteous man,

Had to die for it.

But what?

It was a long time ago and

It's not like I had anything to do with it!

I only reap the benefits.

Erenhardt

Tata has someone he worked with,

Erenhardt.

A *goy*,

A gentile,

Not a Jewish man.

His factory finished the raw materials that Tata produced.

I suppose that without him,

The materials couldn't be sold,

As they were only half done.

He comes one evening and

Knocks on our door.

He is tall and straight like

The spine of a book,

And all of his features look like

They are sitting in just the right place.

If he were a drawing,

I'd hang it on the wall.

Except that he wears

A black Gestapo outfit,

That smells of sadness.

"Herr Adler!" he says.

Tata doesn't open the door

The whole way.

Erenhardt sticks his hand in

The whole way.

"I come in peace, Herr Adler, my friend!"

Tata opens the door to show,

Mama,

Me,

Bubbe,

Zeide,

Chaim,

Sarah,

Danek.

People Erenhardt once knew.

Shriveled.

"You must come with me," Erenhardt says.

"Where to?" Tata asks.

"Hitler is not right, Herr Adler.

He says there is a Jewish look.

But look at you!

Blond hair!

Blue eyes!

Back like an arrow!

You could run a *grosz* down your nose and it wouldn't hit a snag!

Come, let me show you off."

I want to run, to suck Papa back to us.

"But it's after curfew," Tata says.

"No matter."

Herr Erenhardt has always liked Tata.

That is the only thing that keeps our hearts from skittering

All the way across Lodz,

As we wait two hours for

Tata to return.

(Though as it is, our hearts

Escape from our toes and

Slide halfway across the city.)

Two hours later, Tata returns.

In his right hand is

A packet of cacao

Dull, brown, powdered gold.

In his left hand,

A pair of shoes for me.

Erenhardt stands behind him

And I hear him speak to Mama.

"I took him to an SS pub and

Nobody sniffed him out.

I knew it!"

Then he shakes his head, slowly,

Like a sated mosquito.

"I'm very sorry for all of you," he says.

"But you will all be killed."

He takes a step back.

"It has nothing to do with me, though.

It is the regime."

His words

Are the strings that

Tie my dreams together

Long after the clomping of his boots,

Float out into the starry night in Lodz.

Long after I wear these shoes

Down to tiny nubs.

Four Officers

Four officers came to count us.

One, two, three, four.

They were not hard to count.

Neither were we.

One, two, three, four, five, six, seven, eight.

Nine if you counted,

The person Mama is growing.

Counting is a bad thing.

Counting means they are figuring out how many

Of us they need to get rid of.

The next morning,

Before the sun reaches so much as a pinky into the sky,

We leave Zeide's apartment.

Tata stuffs a wheelbarrow,

With the few belongings we have left.

It is March but

There isn't a whiff of spring.

Thick icicles hang from the roofs,

Like frozen beards.

"Where will we go?" Mama asks.

"I know someone. The name is Toyter," Zeide says.

Toyter means a dead person.

I am certain we are going to live,

In a mortuary,

But it is only the family's name.

The kind Toyter family,

Welcomes us inside,

Where our breath can defrost.

Zeide receives the bed of honor,

Atop the table.

I sleep under the table,

Like a dog,

Nestled with my siblings,

My puppies.

The Ghetto

Now, we needed to find a place

But how to move with no money?

No food?

Nothing to offer,

But a pile of burden.

We split up from Bubbe and Zeide Blass,

Them to one side of the ghetto,

Us to another,

Wherever we can find a space

To roost.

The ghetto,

Where the Germans want all of the Jews to be—

Squished together

Like pigeons.

There we find a room on

Zgierska Street 50,

For a pittance.

The room is a pittance.

In the Baluter section,

Where everything is filth

And the streets run with sewage,

Where the moans of the wind mix with

The moans of the people,

And the people are

Louder.

Where withered people,

Stare with

Eyes sitting like buttons

In shrunken heads.

They walk like ghosts,

Bare feet barely touching the earth,

Already halfway to heaven.

The ghetto.

Oh, how the mighty have fallen.

Hungry 2

I thought that the hungry in Pabianice,

Was nothing compared to,

The hungry in Lodz.

But the hungry in Lodz,

Has the neck of a pig, *gevalt*, a non-kosher animal

Compared to the hungry in the Ghetto Lodz,

Which has the neck of a giraffe.

Mama says,

Hunger is something that kills you,

Even before it kills you.

Fear

Sometimes the fear,

The wondering about:

Tomorrow,

An hour from now,

A minute from now,

Now.

Makes you forget the hungry.

Changed My Mind

Nothing can make you forget hungry.

No.

Not even fear.

Dreaming of Bronia

When our cook, Bronia, stood over her pots,

The angels must have danced with joy from the heavenly aromas.

Her chopped liver…

Goose livers and cut onions. Hard boiled eggs hacked to bits. And a thick dollop of *schmaltz*.

When she prepared it my tongue hung from my mouth,

Waiting.

"Please?" I would beg. "Give me a piece!"

"No!"

"But I must have!"

"You will wait."

I went to Mama who was reciting Psalms in the dining room.

"I'm just curious. Whose livers are those, anyway?

Bronia's? Or yours?"

Mama leaned forward.

"You do want that liver, don't you?"

I nodded.

"Well, then, you're going to have to wait!"

Cousin Leibel

Remembering Bronia always leads to—

Cousin Leibel.

That's because whenever Chocha Raizel,

Cousin Leibel's mother, used to call,

Bronia would call out to Mama—

"The *mechuteinister* is on the phone!"

She was sure Leibel and I would marry one day

And Mama and Chocha Raizel would be in-laws.

Remembering this makes me smile.

And wonder—

Could it possibly…

Goodness, how can I think of weddings—

In Ghetto Lodz?

More on Cousin Leibel

Last I saw Cousin Leibel,

He was a terrible child.

He lived far away in Przemyśl.

When he came to visit Pabianice the first time,

 He went around *hocking* and *klopping* any cousin,

Who stood in his way.

When he entered a room,

All the cousins would cluster under the table,

Squishing against the wall,

Trying to make themselves disappear.

Except for me.

One day I lay on the gondola chair in the dining room,

Cousin Leibel took this as an invitation.

WHACK! Did he really just hit me?

Contrary to his belief,

He hadn't been invited.

I gave him a good, sturdy *klop* in return.

He looked at me, blue eyes twinkling.

"Maniusia, you and I will be friends," he said.

And how!

Oh, how I miss Bronia!

Oh, how I miss Cousin Leibel!

But Mama is moaning in the next room

And Tata is calling me.

There is little time for missing,

In Ghetto Lodz.

The Thing That Happens in This Room

The thing that happens in this room is,

We wake up one morning

And the person Mama has been growing,

Has arrived!

Somehow,

In the still of night,

While we slept,

Mama hadn't uttered a peep,

And our brother slithered into the world.

But this baby,

Does not look like a baby at all.

Babies,

Have dimples in their skin,

And pink in their cheeks.

Babies,

Cry like a train whistle,

And tamp the air down with their fists.

This baby,

Is thin as a challah knife,

Bones poking at his sallow skin,

Fingers like grated potatoes,

Slowly unclenching his fist,

Then closing it again,

Like he knows,

There is nothing to receive.

Milk

Sarah begins crying first.

Then me.

Then Chaim.

And Baby Danek.

This is how we tell our new little brother

Welcome to the world.

Mama tries to feed the baby,

One skeleton pressed against another,

"*Gut in Himmel*," she cries.

"Please! Milk for my baby!"

But Mama is a broken faucet.

Not a drop squeezes forth.

And the baby's lips stay dry,

Except for the tears that fall from our eyes,

Onto his brand-new face.

Trapped

Rumors run.

"They're closing the ghetto."

Soon a wire fence goes up,

With silver necklaces on top,

We are chickens in a coop.

Not that we have anywhere to go,

Anyway.

As If

As if it isn't enough to cage us in,

Like chickens,

The wire fence around the ghetto is

Full of electricity.

One touch and

You are fried chicken.

Some people prefer that over

Hungry, scared, hungry.

They cook themselves on that fence,

Handing themselves over to the Germans,

On a platter.

The King

The Germans appoint a head to our ghetto.

Ghetto Lodz.

Not Hans Biebow, the German in charge.

A Jew.

With hair white like eggs,

Thick as porridge,

And a real pair of glasses.

Chaim Rumkowski.

He stands on a podium and

Makes speeches,

His voice is loud,

But I don't dare cover my ears.

"We will work and we will live," he says.

"We will open factories.

There will be school for the children."

That last one,

Makes me think of something

Other than hungry for a moment.

I thirst to learn.

Not nearly as much as I thirst

For purple grape juice,

Sticky on my lips,

But close enough.

Cheers ring out from

The crowds full of

Skinny people,

Like the starved cows you see,

In the mountains.

We cheer for the good king,

Who will prevent our bodies from evaporating.

Who will give us school!

We cheer for King Rumkowski.

School

I miss school like I miss warm comforters.

I loved every breath I took in school.

I'd walk there and I'd sit and have the world,

Handed to me on a dinner plate.

The length and breadth of the earth,

Divided into countries and states and cities and towns,

How our skin covers our bones,

And how the giant planets hover above,

Without plummeting down onto our tiny human heads.

I loved learning even more than—

I loved to misbehave.

Twice a week Naomi Goldberg came to my house after school.

Mama hired her to help expand my intellect.

We talked about many things but mostly books.

Mama used to say that every book is a world.

She said that even in a very bad book, if you tried hard enough,

You would find something good.

My favorite school days were twice a year

When the *visitator* came to check on what the school was teaching us.

The teacher opened her roll book

And called on a student to be tested by the *visitator*.

Guess who was first in the roll book with a last name that begins with an "A"?

I loved when he asked me questions.

Only because I knew the answers.

I decided then and there,

That I must marry someone whose name begins with an "A."

He would have to know all the answers, too,

And our children would *certainly* be smart.

Cousin Leibel's last name starts with an "A."

His last name is the same name as mine.

Just by the way.

Answers

How can it be that

I knew exactly what to say to the *visitator*,

And now,

I have so, so, so many questions,

And not even one teeny-tiny answer?

Maps

King Rumkowski,

Makes a ghetto map.

That way he can assign everyone

To a work detail.

He slices the ghetto into parts,

Like a loaf of bread.

Every few streets is

Its own little country,

Every country divided

Into cities,

Cities into

Towns,

Towns into

Neighborhoods,

Neighborhoods into

Streets,

Streets into

Houses,

Houses into

Families,

Families into

People,

People into,

Nothing at all.

Dethroned

King Rumkowski

Brings work to the ghetto,

But he doesn't bring:

Plums,

Pastries,

Carrots,

Cherries.

Milk for the baby.

He gives bread rations,

To those who work,

Crumbly little pieces.

And sometimes,

A glorious potato to suck on.

We walk around the ghetto like

Piles of moving sticks,

Arms like long strings of licorice,

Legs like skinny yams,

Stomachs swollen

"Like tumors," Mama says.

Sometimes people stop walking.

One minute you see them,

Jerking down the street like

Their fingers are being pulled by strings,

And then they lie down,

In the middle of the filthy street,

Too tired to sew another stitch of life,

They crumple into

A baggy pile of clothing on the ground,

In a shop front,

Or near the septic tanks.

It doesn't matter.

They lie down for a nap and

Never wake up.

People quickly begin wondering

What kind of a king,

Rumkowski is,

His subjects

Dropping like flies.

Odd Jobs

Tata used to work with textiles,

Silks and organzas,

Cottons and tweeds,

Now he is—

He is—

A

Fecalist.

My holy, pious *tata*,

Who always woke just when the sky cracked open,

Morning after delicious morning,

His voice like the plucked string of an instrument,

As he reached for G-d,

Now pulls a cart,

Loaded with human waste,

To earn a few *groszy*,

To earn a loaf of bread for us,

And something for the baby to suckle on.

Does anyone in this ghetto know,

That their sewers are being emptied

By a diamond?

Moving

Tata's messy business,

Doesn't earn enough for the room

At Zgierska Street 50.

"We must move again," Tata says.

His sigh is as long as his face.

"They're opening up another part of the ghetto.

There we can find a room."

The other part of the ghetto,

Where the rooms cost less

Than the old dress on my back.

Tata runs there,

Like there are coals under his toes,

To snag a room—for us.

Our new address?

Brzezinska 86.

Thirty-six units higher than Zgierska 50,

But that's the only thing higher

About Brzezinska 86.

The room has a constant wetness,

That leaches from the walls,

Onto your skin,

And it is dark as an ocean

With only a crescent moon to light it.

Come to think of it,

It is more boat than house,

Dingy and damp.

Only, a boat would be preferable.

A boat could sail us out of here.

Horses

We used to go to the spa every summer—

At Rabka.

It was a bit of heaven in the Polish countryside for children.

Children like us.

We'd take the overnight train to get there

And the peasants would stare from the sides of the road.

At me and my siblings.

At our fancy frocks,

At our baskets packed with oranges,

At our hair yellow as corn.

In Cracow there was a fast train transfer

But Tata used to say that nothing is fast with four children in tow.

But he had an idea.

Some people would request porters to carry their luggage.

Tata took five porters.

One to carry the luggage to the next platform.

The other four to carry us four children.

Tata always had ideas.

In Rabka we drank saltwater,

Took saltwater baths,

And received inhalations,

To prevent tuberculosis—all under a doctor's supervision.

I was a terrible eater and skinny as a railroad track.

At weigh-in, for every kilo that I gained,

I'd get a zloty.

A zloty could buy two chocolate bars!

After weigh-in we rode ponies,

Our legs slapping at their sides,

The wind in my hair,

And my heart felt as light as *wieczorowka*,

The flakiest pastry on this side of the earth.

Mama sent us to the spa because she believed in—

Prevention.

That's why we used to have beautiful legs,

From drinking so much milk,

While most Polish people,

Tottered on sickle-shaped legs.

And our teeth!

Most Poles went to the dentist only when,

Their teeth were nearly tripping out of their heads.

You'd see them on the street with puffed out cheeks and

Bandages wrapped round their faces.

Cousin Leibel and I always tried to guess

Who was underneath.

But Mama took us to Dr. Szapocznick twice a year,

Even when our teeth were firmly planted in place.

Because every part of us was

Important,

Down to the last tooth.

But in Ghetto Lodz,

There is no prevention and

The horses have a different job.

They pull the carts,

That pluck the dead,

From sidewalks,

Streets,

Corners.

Those carts fill faster than,

The carts that used to visit Pabianice,

Selling clothing,

Hats,

Apples.

It isn't just hunger that kills.

The Germans walk around,

Spinning their guns like toys.

They play games.

"That Jew walks like a duck."

Boom! Boom! Dead!

He falls slowly,

First his knees,

Followed by

The unfortunate rest of him.

"That couple looks too happy."

Boom! Boom!

They're not looking happy anymore.

That is why the horses in the ghetto,

Have no sleep

And I imagine their dreams,

Are far less pleasant,

Than the ponies' dreams in Rabka.

A Miracle

I am walking home,

Ha! Home!

To Brzezinska 86,

With my friend Chanchi Blum.

I see something on the street that,

Doesn't look like the usual trash.

I bend my thin frame over to look.

"Chanchi. It's a wallet!"

It is surely empty.

It isn't empty.

Inside that wallet,

Forty-eight marks.

Enough for bread

And potatoes

For a family

For a month.

Inside that wallet,

The ticket to life,

For me,

Mama,

Tata,

Chaim,

Sarah,

Danek,

Skeleton baby.

But also inside the wallet,

Identification.

Someone else's family,

That isn't eating for a month.

Their mama,

Their *tata*,

Their Sarah,

Or Henny,

Or Dovele,

Or Itzik,

And maybe another

Skeleton baby.

The *yetzer tov* and the *yetzer hara*—

The good and the bad parts,

Inside of me, pulling at each other's ears until,

"I'm bringing this to the police," I say.

Chanchi's yellow eyes become

As big as suns.

"That might be

The dumbest thing I've ever heard."

By now,

I've heard way too many dumb things to know,

That this isn't the dumbest one of all.

But I don't argue with her.

She walks two steps behind me,

All the way to the police station.

What My Parents Say

I walk through the door

Of our little, damp boat,

See Mama holding our darling baby,

His head resting like a planet between

His jutting shoulder blades,

See Sarah's blue eyes,

Lakes of hunger,

See Danek's arms,

Like umbrella spokes

And a cry comes out from me,

So loud,

It is like a snowball

That rolls

And rolls

Getting bigger

And bigger

Until it knocks me over.

"*GEVALT!*

I'm so, so, so sorry," I cry.

Mama rushes toward me.

I kiss the baby's sweet forehead.

"What are you sorry for?" Mama asks.

"You've done nothing wrong, *mamele*."

"But I have."

In between gasps,

I tell her the story,

Tata comes in from work in the middle,

Listening.

"And…you could have eaten,

For a month," I say, when I finish telling.

Mama and Tata look at each other,

Then at me.

The hungry children,

Listen.

"You did the right thing," they say.

"We couldn't be more proud of you."

Before

Before this war,

I don't know how much proud,

Mama and Tata had for me.

I was a wild girl.

And when Cousin Leibel visited,

We were wild times two.

Every Saturday was our holy Sabbath;

Shabbos.

On Shabbos afternoons,

When my parents slept,

He and I played train conductor

Dragging all of the dining room chairs to the middle of the room,

Slamming the door of the balcony open and shut,

Not remembering to think of the parents sleeping.

When Tata called out, "Stop with the banging!"

Cousin Leibel only banged harder.

I was a very good accomplice.

One Shabbos we went upstairs to visit,

The rabbi of Pabianice.

I opened up the breakfront,

And made a train of all the silver candlesticks,

Across the length of the room.

Those candlesticks were *muktzeh*,

Which meant you weren't allowed to touch them on Shabbos.

Nobody could walk into the dining room for the rest of the day.

And nobody could walk out.

"What have you done?" Mama cried,

Seeing what I'd done in the home of

The great Rav Menachem Mendel of Pabianice,

Son of the holy Sfas Emes,

A Grand Rabbi from the city of Gur.

But that wasn't all.

Cousin Leibel has a beautiful singing voice.

One day he asked me to accompany him to the courtyard.

Sometimes, people came to sell things.

They'd *handel* old clothing,

Or perform in the hopes of a few *groszy*.

He handed me his hat…

"You will hold this," he said.

"And I will sing."

"And what will I do with the hat?" I asked,

Knowing full well!

"You will collect the money."

And until the adults finally found us,

That is exactly what I did.

No, I don't remember a lot of proud back then.

But I'd take all of Mama and Tata's proud now,

And throw it in the sea,

To go back there.

It Doesn't Help

Mama and Tata's proud,

Doesn't earn Tata more money.

Tata still works as a—

As a—

Fecalist.

People whisper,

That it is only a matter of time,

Before these workers,

Become diseased,

And die,

Like my eighteen-year-old cousin, Chaim Hertzberg,

He should rest in peace.

I watch Tata hauling a wagon of human waste down the street,

Worse than a horse,

And I feel my heart,

Blown to bits,

In a way,

No bomb,

Could ever,

Accomplish.

My Tata.

Chassid of the grand Rebbe of Gur

REB YITZCHAK ADLER!

Cleaning waste pits.

I believe I have finally found something worse,

Than hungry.

Summoned by King Rumkowski

Chanchi Blum and I,

Are called to the office,

Of King Rumkowski.

Apparently,

The police informed him,

Of our returning the wallet,

The wallet that could have saved,

Our sweet, starving baby,

At least for a few weeks.

His office is in the town square,

The Baluter Ring,

Three kilometers from us.

Forget that I am weak,

From hungry,

I do not own a pair of shoes.

(I have long grown out of

Mr. Erenhardt's generous gift.)

My cousin,

Chana Hertzberg,

Angel that she is,

Lends me her precious shoes.

They are one and a half sizes too small for me.

That's how I walk, three kilometers,

With pinched toes

And heels probably growing spurs.

Rumkowski's office is in a beautiful hut,

In a square that used to be a marketplace,

In a neighborhood once considered so decrepit,

Mama wouldn't have let us stick our big toe inside it.

All the bigshots sit in that fenced-in square,

Even the German overseer, Hans Biebow.

Rumkowski's office looks like,

My life on the other side

Of this war.

Before the war,

Rumkowski used to head an orphanage,

People say he

Loves children.

I only hope he will

Love me, too.

Me and Rumkowski

"What made you return that money?"

Rumkowski asks me,

Once we are alone.

"It was another man's wages," I say.

"It was another man's potatoes."

We speak for a time,

Me and the king,

As if it happens,

Every day.

"I see how you look," he says.

"You're a very smart child."

And then he asks me,

"What does your father do?"

I look down

At my cousin's shoes.

"He is a fecalist."

My voice is tiny,

Saying this very big thing.

He bangs on his desk,

Like a judge.

"I can see this upsets you,

Very much

And I can't bear to see

A girl who won't steal

Another man's potatoes,

Cry.

I will move your father to another detail,

In your merit."

The guilt that has been piled,

So high inside me,

It has nearly cut off my breathing passages,

Rolls over then,

And leaves me,

In beads of wet sweat.

Cigarettes All Around

Tata is assigned to

The cigarette detail.

He works at home,

In our one-room boat,

Rolling paper and

Filling it with *tabak*.

I live with cigarette smells,

Twenty hours a day.

My water is cigarette juice.

I sleep with cigarette dreams.

And I am so,

Incredibly,

Grateful.

Nameless Baby

Our baby

Can't be circumcised,

Not on the eighth day,

As Jewish law dictates,

And not in the eighth week.

He is not well enough,

For that kind of thing.

Sometimes,

We get a little milk for him.

In the beginning,

He'd lap it up,

Like a kitten,

But now,

He is too weak,

Even for that.

Sometimes,

We get sugar water,

But it is never enough.

He is shrinking,

Pieces of him leaving us

Every day.

Milk

When we hear they will be distributing milk,

Whole milk,

Frothy as the clouds,

When we read the signs,

We light up.

Every last one of us,

Except the baby,

Who doesn't understand.

The milk will be for him.

But that is enough to bring a sparkle,

To our dark lives.

Mama wakes in the morning,

With a smile,

Left over from her dreams.

We watch the baby.

The baby who still doesn't have a name.

Because he doesn't have a circumcision.

Because he doesn't have health.

Because he doesn't have milk.

This milk,

It will name him.

Mama leaves,

Her arms empty,

Waiting to be filled.

One hour passes.

Then two.

Three.

It is twenty hours.

Before Mama comes back.

Only it isn't the same Mama,

That left in the morning.

New Mama

Mama rolls in slowly,

Like her feet are giant melons.

Her face.

So bruised,

It could be,

An overripe plum.

Her arms look like,

Someone has used them,

To rake the streets,

And her face,

Lined with bruises

Like rows of raisins,

Turning to bulging prunes,

Before our eyes.

Her nose is

Off center and

Blood runs,

From the corners of her eyes,

Crimson tears.

The story is:

The Germans invited mothers,

To come and get milk,

For their skeleton babies.

But they had really been invited,

To a different sort of event.

Instead,

The Germans came on horses

And beat these women,

Until they couldn't remember,

Why they had come at all,

And these women could never remember,

Much of anything the right way,

Ever again.

That's How Much

Like the first lick

Of ice cream.

Like lying in a

Hot bath,

Water lapping at your toes.

Like crispy, curly-edged

Fried potatoes,

Like succulent chicken

Smothered in sauce,

Like going to sleep,

With a stomach swollen with food,

And more than all those things,

That's how much we love

Our baby.

Goodbye

Our beloved baby,

Dies.

It feels like someone has come,

And scooped me out,

Like a gourd.

That's how empty I am

Without him.

Mama hasn't been right in her mind,

Or her body,

Since the Germans bashed at her brains.

But who can say,

What is right in the mind,

Under such circumstances?

She holds our dead baby,

Tightly against her,

Loving him fiercely,

And for the first time,

She can give him everything he needs.

The Circumcision

Tata comes and tries

To pry the baby away.

"We must bury him, Chana," he says,

His voice as soft as a breeze.

She holds our baby closer still.

"I won't let him go," she says.

We wait,

Mama,

Tata,

Sarah,

Chaim,

Danek,

Me,

And our beloved, dead baby.

"I will go and speak to Mr. Klein," Tata says.

Mr. Klein comes downstairs.

He speaks to Mama

And to our baby.

"If you don't bury him,

He will not be able to go to Gan Eden,"

He says.

Mama wants our baby to go to heaven,

After a life that was just the opposite of that.

She wants heaven for our baby even more than

She wants to hold his tiny body,

A crescent moon against her chest.

She lets him go.

Before they bury him,

They find a sliver of glass,

And our baby finally receives,

His circumcision.

And a name.

Avraham Moshe.

After his great-grandfather,

Who lived ninety years,
While our baby never even reached,
Nine months.

School's Out

School in the ghetto
Isn't much to speak of—
But at least it is
Facts and figures,
Numbers and notions,
Peeking through our grimy fingers,
Into a kinder world somewhere.
But honestly,
The best thing about ghetto school,
Is the lunch soup you get every day,
Though "soup" is rather an exaggerated word,
For water with a bit of floating scum on top.
But King Rumkowski says he can't keep up
With the Germans' demands.
They want more workers,
To run their war machine.
Which means that children, too,
Need to work.

Children who work cannot also be
Children who go to school.
Children who work,
The full face of the clock,
Aren't really children.
Are they?

The Saddle Workshop

At the saddle factory,
I sit on a bench,
That molds to my shape,
Even though it is hard as a mountain,
That's how many hours I sit.
At the end of the bench are two slots,
You slip the leather in
And make holes,
With an awl.
Saddles to support German men.
One day the son of a bigshot
In the saddle detail,
Approaches me.
"That's a fine awl you have there,"
He says.

"I'd like an awl like that for myself."

Well, wouldn't he!

I have the finest awl of all.

Tata had traded a piece of BREAD for that awl!

But I have no choice.

His father being a bigshot!

I give him my awl.

From then on,

I have to work twice as hard

To poke holes through the leather.

I'm ashamed to say,

I cry over my stolen awl.

But it isn't all so bad.

After work, a few of us like to perform.

We put on the play,

Locomotive,

And I win the main part!

It is the story of a boy who had tuberculosis.

He didn't make it.

Hmmm.

I suppose the play

Isn't much of an escape,

From real life.

Siberia

In the ghetto,

Each person lives,

For himself.

I lived for six other people.

And now five.

So I don't think much of anyone else.

But when I come home and see Tata

Crying like his eyes might drop out of his head,

And he tells me it's about Feter Beirish and his family,

I nearly throw up my heart.

"They were sent to Siberia," he says.

"It's cold enough there to freeze your breath into icicles,

The moment it leaves your mouth.

The snow is so high,

There are no footprints."

Tata wants to sit *shivah*,

Seven days of mourning,

For his brother.

"Siberia is a land of death," he says.

"There's no hope."

I can't imagine anything worse,

Than where we are now.

But I'm not as worried as Tata is.

I know that Cousin Leibel,

Will find a way to leave his footprint,

Even in Siberia.

The Luxtorpeda

That night I can think of nothing but—

Cousin Leibel,

His *peyos*, his sidelocks freezing like icicles against his cheeks.

I think of Przemyśl—the grandest trip of my life.

Tata was the only one who could put a muzzle on Cousin Leibel.

A few years ago,

A few lifetimes ago,

He promised Leibel that if he'd behave for six months running,

He'd bring me to Przemyśl,

For the wedding of another cousin,

Leibel Hertzberg.

Przemyśl is an overnight train ride away

From Pabianice.

And bringing me,

Was the biggest prize Cousin Leibel could hope for.

I didn't hold my breath.

Six months was a long time to expect good behavior

From any child,

From Cousin Leibel?

Impossible.

They called it a miracle when

Feter Beirish said,

His son Leibel had behaved like a *malach*

A proper angel,

Six months running.

The reward was mine to bask in.

Tata took me to Przemyśl, just us two.

In the Luxtorpeda—a train like a palace,

With our own compartment.

Cousin Leibel and Feter Beirish waited for us at the station.

Leibel knows I love ice cream so

We headed straight for the parlor.

Every day in Przemyśl,

We ate ice cream,

Sticky and dripping tiny rivers on our wrists.

At the wedding, I wore a dress of sea green with a matching beret.

I stood with my mouth as wide as the moon

While I watched men—

Greeting their fathers and brothers and cousins

With kisses,

Like ladies who were the best of friends!
"This is the way it is done in Galicia," Tata said.
Cousin Leibel ran across the wedding hall,
Chased by his mother with a curling iron,
Fighting against nature to twist his sidecurls
Into the desired shape,
But nothing about Cousin Leibel
Could ever be twisted
Into the shape you wanted.

Resettlement

King Rumkowski receives orders
From German kings,
More powerful than him.
Sometimes,
He sends trains full of
The sick,
The elderly,
And those who volunteer
For resettlement,
Away from here.
Where to?
Nobody knows.

But this time,

This time,

This time,

He asks for—

Children.

"Fathers and mothers, give me your children!

I must cut off limbs in order to save the body itself.

I must take the children, because if not,

Others will be taken as well."

The king needs twenty thousand people for

Resettlement.

Twenty thousand children.

This time, you can see the pain

In the eyes of Rumkowski,

The king who loves children.

I look at Tata.

"We will hide," he says.

"We will hide," he says again.

The first time he says it,

He is trying to reassure me.

I think the second time,

He is trying to reassure himself.

Geshperrer

"The *geshperrer* will be tomorrow," Tata says.

His forehead clenched.

When there is a *geshperrer*,

The Germans come down each street,

And they order everyone outside.

Their shouts are so loud

Through their megaphones,

They can give you black and blue marks,

Calling, calling, calling,

For everyone to leave their homes.

When the people come down,

The Germans pluck,

Children from the arms of their parents,

And elderly parents from the arms of their children.

They take them away.

They never come back.

If you don't leave your home,

They will find you,

Searching,

Building by building,

Room by room,

For every. Last. One.

This *geshperrer* is going to be the worst one of all.

"Which Jew will hand over his child?" Tata asks.

"Rumkowski has asked the unthinkable.

We must hide now."

My aunt, Chocha Hertzberg's, landlord,

Has a hiding room.

A door,

Covered by a giant wardrobe.

We go there.

Tata,

Mama,

Me,

Chaim,

Sarah,

Danek.

And thirty-four other people.

Stuffed in one room,

Like clothing in a wardrobe

For two weeks,

While around us,

The world tears

On a seam.

The megaphones scream in my ears.

EVERYBODY OUT!

HIDING IS PUNISHABLE BY DEATH!

WE WILL FIND YOU!

Every cry outside,

Is a child,

Torn from his mother's arms.

And we can't even think of them,

With how busy we are,

Thinking of ourselves.

For two weeks we hide,

Risking our lives on occasion,

To go out for bits of food.

For two weeks,

Mama feeds us,

And does not feed herself,

Not even a morsel.

For two weeks we cannot

Open our mouths to speak,

Not even a whisper.

And when the German dogs come sniffing,

We try to cover our human scent,

Tucking ourselves into corners.

I hear their barks,

See the fear clawing at everyone's eyes,

I hold tight to Mama's hand.

If they find us,

We will be separated.

Without my family,

I would be a leaf

Fallen off a tree,

I would be nothing.

But the dogs leave,

Wagging their pencily tails,

And we survive,

For now.

New Jobs

I get a new job

At the straw workshop.

There I braid straw all day.

The straw has to be soft,

To make the braids,

So we plunge the straw,

Into icy water,

Followed by our hands.

At first we feel our hands,

But that water is so cold.

Eventually,

You forget that you have hands at all.

Those braids are used

To make overboots for the German soldiers,

In cold places,

Like Russia.

Our frozen hands,

Warm German feet.

Mama

After the beating that

Mama receives,

Trying to get milk for our baby,

She is half in this world,

And half somewhere else.

I am happy enough,

To have half of her.

But with a broken body,

A broken soul,

And no food to fix those things,

Mama doesn't have much of a chance.

I am working in the straw workshop,

When they come running for me,

"Maniusia, you must come immediately.

Your mama is not well.

Not well at all."

I know that this means,

I am going home,

To say goodbye,

To my beautiful mama.

I have to get a pass,

From the head of the detail,

Which takes some time,

And by the time I get home,

Mama is already gone.

"She was waiting for you," Tata cries.

"She didn't want to die,

Without saying goodbye."

But I needed a pass to leave,

Because braiding straw,

Is more important,

Than saying goodbye to my mama.

Mama!

On the twenty-fifth day of the Jewish month of Cheshvan,

In the year 1942,

Mama returns her sweet soul,

To her Creator.

Tata tears his coat in mourning,

A jagged line across his heart,

And my heart is torn, too.

I didn't get to say goodbye to Mama,

So I will say it now.

Goodbye, Mama!

Goodbye, Mama!

Goodbye, Mama!

After Mama

After Mama dies,

I become a mother, too.

A mother to:

Chaim,

Sarah,

And Danek.

Tata no longer works at home.

He's been moved to the Schneider workshop.

He tailors uniforms,

For Nazi soldiers,

So they can be dressed

To kill.

Chaim works too now.

He is a big boy

Of nearly twelve.

He carries nails for the shoemakers,

In the Schuster workshop.

The other children wait at home,

For me.

It is winter and

The cold licks at your insides.

When I come home each day,

The fine hairs on my siblings' cheeks stand at attention,

Frozen hairs,

You can break off like icicles.

Zeide Blass

I did not know that while my mother

Was dying,

Her father was dying

On the other side of the Ghetto Lodz.

There is no transport,

In the ghetto,

Not even your feet,

Without shoes.

I always thought,

You'd be able to feel when

Someone you love

Left the earth,

Like a piece of you would

Go with him.

I suppose in Ghetto Lodz,

If that would be true,

There'd be nothing left,

Even of the people

Left behind.

Shoes

If there is one thing I want

Nearly as much

As a pot of chicken soup,

With golden *kneidlach* floating,

Like buoys,

It is a pair of shoes.

My feet are as black,

As the galoshes I wish I had,

And a crust has formed on my soles,

Like old bread,

Out a week in the sun.

My soles are pocked with

Pebble marks,

And the ache goes

All the way up my shins,

Maybe all the way up

To my teeth.

When Mama dies,

Tata takes Mama's snakeskin valise.

He gives it to Ogo'rek,

Who knows how to make things,

Out of other things.

(The valise,

That Tata had used as a carrier,

To bring Danek all the way to Lodz,

On his back.)

Ogo'rek snips the valise into bits,

And makes me—

A pair of shoes!

I feel like,

I am walking on clouds

And now,

In more ways than one,

I have filled Mama's shoes.

Winter

Which is worse?

Hungry?

Or Freezing?

Hungry makes you mad,

Freezing makes you sad.

Hungry rips at your insides,

Freezing tears at your outsides.

Hungry plays with your brain,

Freezing makes you insane.

Poetry of the Ghetto Lodz.

Mud

When the snow melts,

It leaves behind a world full of mud.

The horses trudge through that mud,

And so do the people.

Lifting the hems of their skirts

And plucking their feet from the muck

Squoosh, squoosh, squoosh.

In Egypt, we learned,

That G-d turned the world to blood,

In Ghetto Lodz,

He turns it to mud.

The mud in Ghetto Lodz is the sort,

That when you slap it,

It slaps you back,

Leaving five fingers on your ankles,

And another few poking into your shoes,

Like soggy bread,

If you are lucky enough to have shoes, that is.

Walking in mud feels

Like sticking your feet inside someone's mouth

Being swished around from cheek to cheek,

Then spit back out,

Slimy and exhausted from the ride.

Gypsies

It is said that the holy Temple of long ago,

Our precious Beis Hamikdash,

Swelled to fit in,

Everyone who came to pray there.

The Ghetto Lodz,

Does not expand,

But still the Germans squeeze more and more people,

Into its tiny space.

When the gypsies come,

With their strange clothing

And their strange ways,

We are moved from our boat,

To the other side of the street.

Towianskiego 6.

The room there is even smaller,

But I work hard,

To make it into a home.

Tata hangs partitions,

To make rooms,

The size of thimbles.

The children have two shirts which

I wash and iron each day,

When I come home from work.

When Mama died,

I got her coat and

From this coat,

I snip and sew,

A coat for Sarah, too.

Each day I clean the floors,

The walls,

The corners of the room,

So that disease has

No surface to grow on

And I cook!

My aunt, Chocha Hertzberg's, landlord

Has a stove.

I take whatever I have to cook with—

A few potato peels,

A moldy piece of turnip,

And I walk there,

In my new shoes.

Later, I come back with

A potful of soup

Covered with a big brown tarp.

The food finishes cooking,

In that bag.

I work all day,

Until I can't bend my fingers,

And then at night,

I work those fingers harder,

Stitching,

Stirring,

Serving,

Scouring.

I used to be dressed by a governess,

Her nimble fingers threading my buttons.

Perhaps I was spoiled,

But I still don't think that

I deserve this.

***Erholung* 1**

People speak of

An *erholung*,

A place where children can go to rest,

Sponsored by King Rumkowski.

There,

Children can eat until

Food fills them,

From their toes

To their hair.

A place like this,

In the Ghetto Lodz,

To rehabilitate,
The children.
King Rumkowski,
He loves his children.
"Maniusia," Tata says,
As I stir a pot of
Potato peel soup.
"I've secured you a place in the rest home.
You need some rest.
For one week, my precious child,
You will live."
I can't imagine,
A week of living.
I want to imagine it.
But looking at the faces of:
Chaim,
Sarah,
Danek,
The dark circles under their eyes…
"Mama, we're so happy for you,"
They say.
I can't imagine a thing.

Erholung 2

Tata manages,

To talk some sense into me.

"If you go to the rest home,

The children can eat your rations,

For an entire week."

This gives me energy.

And so I go.

At the rest home,

The food comes in mountains.

And I remember,

How it feels to be full.

The beds are soft,

With quilts,

Quilts!

Filled with feathers,

And I remember,

How it feels to be warm.

At the *erholung*,

I rehabilitate.

But I miss the children!

I miss them like—

Like a mother.

And I can't help feeling,

That every spoonful that I eat,

I am stealing,

From their sweet, little mouths.

Ode to the Potato Peel

Oh, potato peel.

You used to be,

Scraped into the trash,

Skinny worms,

Caked in earth.

But now you have become,

As desired as a fat turkey,

Swimming laps in a gravy lake.

You are plucked from garbage heaps,

By eager fingers,

Tossed into empty pots,

Boiled in water,

Making skinny potato peel soup.

You are baked into

Potato peel cakes,

You are licked,

Like a lollipop.

Potato peel,

I cannot imagine a time when,

I didn't appreciate,

All that you can be.

A New Job

"Maniusia," Tata says,

When I come home from work,

One gray day,

When the *erholung* is,

A distant memory.

"I have found you a new job."

His eyes shine like stars so,

I figure this is good news.

"You will work in the Schneider workshop," he says.

"With me."

I am a bit frightened of

The sewing workshop.

You see,

Back in school I used to be quite wild.

I played soccer in the gym with all the boys and

Chaim used to say that I was really the boy and he the girl.

(Impossible! I'd tell him. I loved a long, quiet curl-up with a book way too much

And I was the winner of a beauty pageant!)

But we had an hour of recreation where,

The girls learned sewing and

The boys built birdhouses with hammer and nails.

I wanted to build a birdhouse instead!

Now, at the Schneider workshop,

I realize those sewing lessons in school,

Would have come in handy.

They certainly don't need any birdhouses

In Ghetto Lodz.

Luckily,

I am a natural.

At the Schneider workshop,

My fingers aren't plunged,

In icy water.

But that isn't the best part.

At the Schneider workshop,

Tata and I walk to work together,

Every frigid morning.

Tata is in charge of distributing things,

To the workers in every department.

At the Schneider workshop,

I come to Tata every day,

To pick up my sewing notions.

Even if I am sewing socks for

Dirty German feet,

Seeing Tata at work every day,

Is worth it.

The Bacias

The Bacias live in our building.

But they enter,

From the other side.

They are a young couple,

So beautiful.

She was a teacher.

I see her once, leaving,

Her hair covered with a blue bonnet,

Her eyes darting.

"Mrs. Bacia," I cry.

Her head jerks back like

I've socked her under her chin.

"I'm sorry,

I didn't mean to frighten you,"

I say,

Out of breath as I reach her.

"Teacher," I say,

"Tell me something in English."

Mrs. Bacia smiles.

"Why English?"

"Because it's a language I don't know,

But I want to know."

She smiles again, showing all her teeth.

"Good morning," she says.

I bite my lip.

"That sounds like *gut morgen*."

"Very good!" Mrs. Bacia says.

Now I smile, showing all of *my* teeth.

"Your first English lesson," she says.

Target Practice

The Bacias have big problems.

Their entrance to the building,

Has two German guards,

Standing sentry over it.

When the guards tire of standing still,

They like to shoot their guns,

And see where the bullets land,

The way a child would,

Send a stream of spit,

Out into the universe,

Without caring whom it might wet.

Sometimes,

They shoot at the Bacias,

To see what will happen.

When Tata hears about this he says,

"This can't happen.

We will make them an entrance through our room."

Our thimbly room?

With barely enough room to fit the five of us,

Lying side by side,

Like piano keys?

But Tata cuts a door in our room,

Losing an entire wall that we could have

Perched upon.

"Our Sages say," Tata says,

"Whoever saves one Jewish life,

It is as if he has saved an entire universe."

Schedule

It's not like,

We don't have a schedule!

The day starts at night,

When Tata comes home from work,

At seven.

First he finds a *minyan*, a quorum of men,

To pray the evening prayers with.

Then, if we have what to eat,

We call it dinner.

After dinner we wash the children,

With water brought in from outside,

And warmed.

After dinner, I iron their clothes,

With a stone,

Warmed on the fire.

Then I search for pieces of wool

And knit together whatever I can,

To ward off the cold,

A cold so cold,

It eats people.

Tata learns then,

From whatever holy books he has left,

Or he fixes things.

He is always fixing things,

The window,

The floor,

In our broken down room.

He takes our one room and

Makes it into many.

One space for sleeping,

The bedroom!

One space for cooking,

The kitchen!

One space with a bucket that

Tata empties every evening,

The lavatory!

While Tata learns or fixes,

I can't help but feel a little bit proud,

Me,

Who couldn't button her own frock,

Working her calloused fingers

Halfway till morning,

Getting things ready,

For another day.

How the Days Pass

How does a day pass?

Morning

Afternoon

Evening

Sleep.

Morning

Afternoon

Evening

Sleep.

That's how

The days,

The months,

The years pass.

In the Ghetto Lodz.

Looking for Tata

Our room is very popular,

People knock all night long,

While Tata fixes,

Or learns,

Looking for him.

"Did you hear the news?" they ask him.

"What do you think we should do?"

There are no radios in Ghetto Lodz,
Only words buzzing from people's mouths,
Carrying rumors like leaves on a breeze.
All evening long they come,
"Reb Adler! What do you think of this?"
Hoping to jump into his holy brain,
For answers,
Answers,
Answers.

The Crazy Man

"Did you hear?"
"Could it be true?"
"He is not of sound mind."
A man comes to Ghetto Lodz,
Spreading rumors,
But these rumors are different.
These rumors are like birds,
Wearing sacks so heavy,
They
CRASH
To the ground.
"When they come and they take people,

In the Ghetto Lodz,"

The crazy man says,

"I will tell you where the people go."

Tata says the man's eyes were wild,

Like deer running,

From the butt of a hunter's rifle.

"They take them to a place,

Where the dogs bark all night,

And flames stuff the sky,

With human ash.

Those humans that are gathered here,

Are deposited there,

And pushed into chambers,

That fill with gas,

And choke the life out of them.

Then they are incinerated,

By the hundreds,

Or maybe the thousands.

I know.

I escaped from there."

The knocks on our door that night,

Come often,

And loud,

Everyone wondering at this man,

This man who must be crazy.

Their eyes look to Tata.

He shakes his head slowly.

"Poor *mentsch*," he says.

"He speaks of a factory,

Where they manufacture,

Death.

Impossible."

New Shipments

The Ghetto Lodz,

Keeps on getting shipments.

Not of bread.

Not of cabbage.

Shipments of people.

First the Gypsies.

Then the Jews.

Jews from Czechoslovakia.

Wrapped in fur stoles,

With cheeks as fat as apples,

Carrying snakeskin valises,

Like the one Mama brought here,

So many centuries ago,
At least that's how it feels.
They look around at the Ghetto Lodz,
Like they've gotten their foot stuck,
In the lavatory,
And they can't figure out,
Whom to call to unstick it.
They look at us,
Like we are rats,
Poking our noses,
Out of that lavatory.

The Ghetto Carousel

When the Czech Jews first came,
Blinking, blinking,
Not believing,
There was room for them—
We were already stacked like fence posts.
But now,
With every shipment in,
There is a shipment out,
The ghetto like a pitcher spilling drops.
There are no *geshperrers* anymore.

Instead, there are lists.

Lists for the next shipment out.

Lists of people.

Each morning the people gather

Near the train station,

In a big square.

For

Resettlement.

The Germans say,

"Bring your tools!

Bring what you have!

Bring your clothing!

There will be work!

In this new place!

In this Resettlement."

But we smell a rat.

When your name is called,

You shiver in your shoes,

Or in your bare feet if you have none.

You don't know what resettlement means,

But you don't like the thought of it.

Not one bit.

Every day more and more leave,

Resettling,

And Tata and I wonder,

As people come in

And people go out,

On the ghetto carousel,

When it will be our turn.

Feter Yankel

Tata buttons his coat and pulls me aside.

"There is a transport of people,

In the—

In the—

The—

Prison."

His eyes are wide,

His words are wide.

"I have word that Feter Yankel is among them."

I nod.

I know Tata will go.

He will do whatever he can,

To save the uncle,

Who saved us.

But Tata comes back later,

His face as long as his shadow.

He curls up in his bed

And he cries into the night,

For the brother he loves,

Whom he will never see again.

A Knock

Our door is knocked upon

Enough times,

To know the difference between,

A knock

And a KNOCK.

A knock is shy.

If a knock could speak it would say,

"Excuse me,

I don't mean to interrupt,

Can you help me?"

A KNOCK has its fists up,

It is persistent,

It lands right in the middle,

Of your forebrain.

If a KNOCK could speak,

It would say,

"Let me in.

Or I'll huff

And I'll puff,

And I'll blow

Your house down."

That's the kind of KNOCK we get,

This evening.

The Kripo

We have no choice,

But to let them in.

The Kripo.

The Criminal Police.

Who is the criminal?

Danek in his too small pajamas?

Sarah, sucking on her thumb like a carrot?

It is Tata they are looking for.

"You will come with us," they say.

First,

They search our room,

Under the mats,

In the corners,

How long does it take to search a home,

The size of a mouse?

Then they tug Tata's arms

And his legs.

"*Schnell*! Out!" they yell.

He looks over his shoulder at me,

Sad,

Angry,

Helpless,

Frustrated.

I've already learned not to beg.

It only makes you feel,

More of an animal,

Than you've already become.

"What will happen to Tata?"

The children ask,

After he's gone.

"Oh, he'll be back soon," I say.

I say *Shema Yisrael*, the bedtime prayer, with Danek.

I tuck in Sarah.

I wash Chaim's clothing for tomorrow.

Then I lie in bed,

My eyes open and unblinking,

The silver moon lighting up the cracks on the ceiling,

Every one of them shaped like Tata.

Ode to Tata

Who else is like you, Tata?

I will never forget how,

You searched the ghetto for

A doctor to help me with things

Most motherless girls would

Have been left to deal with,

Alone.

I will never forget how,

You walked three miles,

When your ribs nearly poked

Through your skin,

And your shoes were more hole

Than shoe,

To tell Cousin Tema,

To stay home from work,

That they'd be rounding up people,

At the rug factory where she worked.

You didn't tell me,

You were going to save her life,

But she did.

I will never forget

All of the unforgettable

Things

About

You.

But

After three days without Tata,

Three days without sleep,

Three days of answering the children's questions,

Questions I have no real idea,

How to answer,

One and a half days of

Knowing inside

That Tata will never

Come back.

Tata.

Comes.

Back.

Gems

His face

Flecked with red,

That runs down his face,

Onto his clothing.

His cheeks,

Two tomatoes,

Dripping seeds.

"They wanted my jewels," Tata tells me.

"Ha! They wanted my diamonds,

My pearls,

My rubies!"

He spreads his arms,

Wincing in pain,

"You four,

Are the only gems I have left."

What Your Books Say

Later,

Tata tells me,

What they did.

"They told me,

It says in your holy books,

That a befitting punishment,

Is forty lashes.

Can you believe

How educated they are

In our traditions?

The only difference is,

I committed no crime.

But that didn't matter.

They beat me until,

I was half dead.

But in the eyes of G-d,

There is no such thing as half dead.

And so,

I am alive."

I will take

Any percentage of Tata,

Alive.

On G-d

The Germans think that they know

What our holy books say,

But our holy books are holier,

Than their holy of holies.

They don't know what it means to taste,

The nectar of Torah.

Mama went to great lengths to make sure,

That her daughter studied Torah, too.

She knew that school could feed our minds,

Leaving our souls

Thirsty.

With her friend Rivtcha Horowitz,

She founded the Bais Yaakov in Pabianice,

Where Jewish girls could learn Torah studies,

After mornings spent learning the world.

Sarah Schenirer came to our house and took me on her knee,

Near our massive living room table.

She had come to discuss the Bais Yaakov with Mama.

I didn't even know that she was famous,

For bringing Torah learning to Jewish girls all over Europe.

I didn't know how people had cried in disbelief,

When they heard that she was coming to Pabianice,

All the way from Cracow.

I only knew the feel of her cheek

Against the top of my head.

Sarah Schenirer who had no children,

Other than every Jewish girl

On the continent.

And I remember how Mama and Tata

Commissioned the writing of a *sefer Torah*,

Because there is a special commandment,

To write your very own,

Torah scroll.

A Torah scroll could cost,

As much as two years' rent.

But our parents ordered a scroll!

The first letters of the holy scroll were inked

At a grand celebration near our home,

In honor of the extension Tata made on our building.

A *chanukas habayis*.

The entire Warszawska Street joined the festivities.

The son of the Rebbe of Gur,

Reb Moshe Betzalel,

Came all the way from Gur!

The chassidim lined the streets,

Dancing,

Twirling,

Singing,

All the way to our apartment.

I held Mama's hand,

And with the other hand,

I held a fistful of sugar lollies.

The children and I sucked them for hours,

And our tongues were still green,

The next morning.

So if you wonder, about me and G-d,

G-d,

Whom I still pray to three times a day,

In the midst of Ghetto Lodz,

With love,

Remember that,

I have so many sweet memories of Him,

To turn in my mind at night.

Speaking of My Mind at Night

Sometimes I dream of Cousin Leibel,

Defrosting his hands in Siberia,

Two melting blocks of ice.

Sometimes I dream of Bronia's chicken soup,

The smell of dill has me clawing at my mattress.

But they say dreams are made of what you hope for

When you're awake,

And usually I dream of,

Nothing at all.

The Shipments Continue

Some of the shipments in,

Are from small towns,

Towns the Germans haven't gotten to yet,

They've been so busy

Killing Jews somewhere else.

Some of the shipments in,

Bring family.

Some,

Bring news.

Some,

Bring stories.

Like that of our old neighbor

Mr. Zelochowski,

He should rest in peace.

Ode to Mr. Zelochowski

Ode to Mr. Zelochowski

Whom they hanged in Kalisz.

Who didn't know you?

You sang like your throat

Was oiled with incense,

From the heavenly altar.

One couldn't listen to you sing,

With his eyes open,

Or his heart closed.

When they hanged you,

(For what offense?

Who even remembers?)

The Germans made people stand

And listen,

As you sang,

Your final repentance,

You cried *vidui*.

"Oh, G-d,

May death be an atonement for all of my errors

And sins."

They said your voice,

Was like a needle,

Poking the heavens,

And that the tears that fell,

Before the noose tightened,

Around your neck,

Could have filled,

The main square

In Ghetto Lodz.

Goodbye, Mr. Zelochowski.

We will miss your very special

Instrument.

Chaim's *Tefillin*

While the carousel turns round

And round,

Shipping in and

Shipping out,

We continue,

With our schedule.

But something big is

Coming up.

Chaim's bar mitzvah.

A bar mitzvah is,

When a Jewish boy turns thirteen,

And begins performing

All of the commandments—mitzvos.

It is the time when a boy,

Begins to wear phylacteries,

Tefillin,

Straps on his arms and

On his head,

With small black boxes,

Full of the holiest words,

Pressed into parchment,

Inside.

There are no *tefillin*,

In Ghetto Lodz.

Not even in its hidden corners.

And my brother Chaim,

Wants them,

More than a piece of

Golden, buttery crumb cake.

One evening,

Tata comes home from work.

"Chaim!" he cries.

"Look what I have for you!"

We all run to see,

What Tata has brought.

Our eyes as big as yarmulkes,

When we see—

The *tefillin*.

Long black leather straps,

And boxes inscribed,

With the Name of G-d.

We touch them gingerly, like they are made of the thinnest glass.

"How did you get them?"

The four of us ask Tata,

A thousand questions,

Or just about that.

Tata smiles.

He puts a finger to his lips.

"Shhhhhhhh.

Just take them.

Bless them.

Wear them.

Live them."

These last two words,

He says to Chaim,

With eyes wide open,

Seeing everything.

His eyes are like drills,

Trying to bore his words,

Into Chaim's soul.

There is so much hope,

In those words,

And with Tata's miracle,

Of finding *tefillin*,

You could almost start to feel

Hopeful, too.

Crunched Up Hope

But it is hard to hope,

In the Ghetto Lodz.

Things get worse.

More soldiers play

More target practice games,

And a new game they like,

Catching people in the streets,

For this or that "sin"

And making an example of that

Unfortunate Jew.

And hungry.

So much very, very, hungry.

If that *tefillin* gave us hope,

It is crunched up fast.

Empty Ghetto

The shipments out,

Go faster than,

The shipments in.

Some new arrivals,

Don't have time to

Unpack their leather valises
Before
They are resettled.
The ghetto looks like
A mouth with too many
Pulled teeth.
Rotting gums left behind.
We live in those gums,
Tata and I look at each other,
With a deep knowing.
"Soon," he whispers.
"Soon."

Our Turn

Four years.
Four years in Ghetto Lodz.
Four years of dodging:
Bullets,
Disease,
Lashes,
Hungry.
Four years of:
Morning

Afternoon

Evening

Night

Work,

Work,

Work,

Work.

And now it is our turn for

Resettlement.

August 21, 1944.

I came to the ghetto eleven years old,

One hundred years old.

I am leaving the ghetto sixteen years old,

Two hundred years old.

The ghetto is so very empty,

One can actually imagine,

Stretching out his legs.

But we are going,

Leaving Mama's bones behind.

Our baby's bones behind.

Where are we going?

Could it

Possibly

Be

Better

Than

Here?

Wondering

Where are we going?

I hear it's better

On the other side.

Of whatever this is.

Anything has to be better

Than this.

It certainly can't,

Be worse.

The Train Station

We arrive at the train platform,

Me holding close

My three most

Precious items,

Sarah,

Chaim,

Danek.

Tata holding,

A sheaf of papers,

I've never seen before.

Chaim holding,

His *tefillin*,

Close against his heart.

People mill,

Wondering,

Asking,

Hoping,

Praying.

A man we know

As a plumber,

Drops his satchel of tools.

A German soldier yells at him,

"Pick it up!

You will need those tools,

Where you are going."

The soldier's words,

Lift us up.

When a Nazi approaches,

We squeeze together,

Trying to hide

In the open air.

The German soldier,

Lays his gloved hands under Danek's armpits,

Lifts him high,

Stares at his face.

"Never," the German says in wonder.

"Never have I seen such a beautiful child."

Then he puts him down gently

And points us toward the trains.

The Talk

When the children sit to rest,

Tata pulls me to the side,

His eyes serious.

"Maniusia," he says.

"We must talk."

I see in Tata's eyes,

That these words will be the most important,

That ever leave his mouth,

To me.

(But I am wrong.)

He hands me the papers in his arms.

"These papers are letters,

From the Rebbe of Gur.

Personal letters,

That he wrote to me.

There is nothing more precious.

And—

The deed to our house

And an insurance package,

That I bought.

After the war,

This could be valuable to you."

"But—you should hold them!" I cry.

Tata lays his hand on my cheek.

"I don't know—"

He stops talking and looks up

At the sun.

Then swallows.

"I don't know who will survive,

Until the end.

But I know for sure,

That you will make it.

That is why I'm giving these treasures,

To you,

My sweet one."

I am still small,

Even at sixteen.

Who could grow much,

On four years of potato peel soup?

So I cling to Tata,

Like a tiny child,

Breathing him in

And then holding my breath,

So that he will remain,

A part of me.

PART 3

THE CAMPS
August 1944–May 1945

Train Ride

On the train,

Meant for cattle,

Not humans,

We sit

Tata,

Me,

Sarah,

Chaim,

Danek.

Chocha Hertzberg.

Her daughter Rivtcha.

Chocha Chana Hendel.

Cousin Mula.

We stand squeezed together,

Our breaths mingling,

Our parched tongues

Licking our cracked lips.

I can't help remembering,

The Luxtorpeda,

That brought me to Przemyśl with Tata,

Such elegance!

Now,

Our bones rattle,

As the train moves,

And people groan,

From hungry

And now a new thing—

Thirsty,

That squeezes the juice from your soul.

At the top of our car,

Is a boarded up hole,

To the outside.

Tata manages to pry open the board.

He pokes his head through

And he calls to the Jewish workers

Standing at the sides of the tracks.

"Where are we going?" he asks them.

"Don't go!" they shout back.

"They will kill everyone over there!

Turn back!"

What foolish advice.

As if we are the train conductors.

As if we can turn back.

As if we are something more than

Cattle.

Doors Open

The doors to the train open,

Letting in a rush of fresh air,

Mixing with the smell of

Unwashed people.

I hear the barking of dogs.

So loud you think,

They are in your head.

Right away,

My heart nearly trips over itself,

Remembering the man,

The crazy *mentsch*,

Who told us about,

The factory of death,

With the barking dogs.

"Raus! Raus!"

The Nazi soldiers,

Also bark like dogs.

"Don't take anything from the trains!

NOTHING!

LEAVE EVERYTHING BEHIND!"

The plumber,

Leaves his satchel of tools.

Chaim,

Leaves behind his *tefillin*,

Like an amputated limb.

I,

Leave all of Tata's precious papers.

But not before I get a good look,

At the name of the insurance policy.

Just in case.

With sticks,

And dogs,

And whips,

The Nazis take us bedraggled passengers,

Off the train.

I hold tight to

My children,

And they to me.

We stand,

In a field packed with dirt,

I see two lines in front of me,

A German soldier at the head of it,

And a German doctor

With a finger like

A lightning bolt,

Pointing left,

Right,

Left,

Right.

Mengele,

The name is whispered,

In fear

And a certain awe,

That makes my stomach ache.

Families split down the middle,

By his long finger,

And those who dare go left,

When called right,

Or right,

When called left,

Are silenced,

With a quick bullet.

The screams of the Jews,

And the dogs,

And the Nazis,

Are like one giant soup.

You can't tell one,

From the other.

I am too scared,

To savor these last moments,

With the people I love,

Too scared to think

Of anything at all.

Leaving

Too soon,

What is left of our family,

Approaches this man,

Whose eyes are not eyes.

How can they be eyes?

If he saw what he was doing,

Then surely

He would stop.

But those eyes look at me,

At Tata

Points us to the right,

Then at

Sarah,

Chaim,

Danek,

Points them to the left.

Those

EYES

Can
NOT
Be
EYES.
That
FINGER
Can
NOT
Be
A
FINGER.
That
DEMON
Can
NOT
Be
A
Man.
The children
Look
At me
At Tata
Such

Beautiful

Faces

Leaving

Me.

In the deepest part of me,

I know,

It will be—

Forever.

"Mama!" they call.

Danek reaches toward me.

Chaim tries to be strong.

I could run after them,

Swallow a bullet,

Meet my end,

Together with them.

But what if I am wrong?

Maybe,

Maybe,

Maybe,

They are going somewhere

Better

Than

Here?

I don't believe that.

Not for one second

But my feet stay planted.

I don't know why.

Goodbye

I watch my children go,

With their Cousin Mula

And Chocha Hertzberg,

Walking toward a chimney,

That spews black ash,

And I try not to remember,

The crazy *mentsch*,

And the workers near the train tracks.

But my insides churn,

My teeth clatter in my head,

And I don't know if,

I can survive another hour,

Let alone till the end of this war.

Only moments after losing the children,

They separate between men and women.

"Tata!" I cry,

As they lead me away,

From my everything.

To the Barracks

They lead us

To wooden barracks,

Me,

Alone,

Empty,

And no comfort to be found,

In the empty people around me.

Will I ever see my family again?

I can't stand.

I can't sit.

I can't BE.

I don't even want to BE anymore.

And then,

Like the miracle worker he always was,

Tata appears,

In the women's barracks.

I think I must be,

Losing my mind,

But he speaks and

He is real.

"Maniusia!" he cries.

"Tata!"

I sob.

"I can't, I can't go on.

Not like this.

Not without the children.

I'm going to kill myself."

Tata grabs me.

"That is why I came, my daughter.

Listen to me.

I will tell you three things.

And then I must go."

I look at my Tata and I know.

This, will be the most important thing,

He ever says to me.

He puts his hands on my shoulders.

"You will never kill yourself, Maniusia.

That is the first thing.

You will always remember who you are and where you came from.

That is the second thing.

And I love you.

That, *mamele*, is the last thing of all."

I shake my head.

"But I can't."

"Promise me, Maniusia!"

"But how?"

"Promise me."

I look at Tata.

At his face waiting for promises,

Because he has,

Nothing else to wait for.

I think of these words,

The most important ones,

He has ever said.

But where will I find the strength to promise something

As big as this?

I reach with everything I have,

Inside the emptiness that is me

And this is what I find.

There is a place inside of me

Underneath all of the places inside that I already know.

In this place, things hide,

Treasures I don't even know I own,

Strength that I carry around with me

Every morning, afternoon and night.

This is the place that I discover,

This is the place from which I pull out these three words:

"I—promise—you."

I will never kill myself

And I will always remember where I came from.

His face relaxes.

"I must go now."

He looks at me one last time

And I at him

And then,

He is gone.

One Last Time

The German soldiers,

Never seem to stop shouting.

"*Schnell! Schnell!*"

If we don't move fast enough,

Their whips are mightier even

Than their screams.

When we are bare

And shivering hard,

They march us to the showers.

On the way to the showers,

I see Tata,

One last time.

I should turn away,

When I see him,

Being whipped,

As he heads to the showers,

Like a horse.

Schnell! Schnell!

I should look away,

So as not to see my strong Tata

Being broken to bits,

A picture,

Drawn in my mind,

Forever,

But I can never look away

From my Tata.

Showers

The water that comes from the showers,

Is cold enough to chill fresh fish,

But at least it is water,

And not gas.

I try to rub my pain away,

With the small bit of soap they give me,

Not that it works.

When we finish,

A line of women who stand with scissors,

And razors.

They cut our hair.

And then shave our heads.

They give us "clothing."

I receive an old sack,

Used for potatoes,

As a skirt,

And an old pajama top.

If I would be thinking straight,

I might find it funny.

Mama used to send Panna Zuzia to Warsaw,

Each year,

To check out the latest fashions,

So that we children,

Would look up to date.

Imagine what she'd think,

If she saw me now,

My head like an egg,

Wearing vegetable sacks.

They stand us in rows of five,

And begin to walk us,

With soldiers all around,

And all of us bald and ugly,

We are animals,

Who need no leashes.

On the side of the road,

There is a broken glass,

In which I can see my reflection.

I am third in the row,

And I have to count,

To figure out which one,

Is me.

Shoes

For four years,

I thirsted for,

Shoes.

Sandals.

Boots.

Clogs.

I wasn't choosy.

Every pair I received,

Was worn to shreds.

That first night in Auschwitz,

They herd us into the barracks,

Like cows.
But they hand me a treasure,
A pair of wooden shoes.
Not that they are my size.
Not that they are comfortable.
Or warm.
But they are shoes.
Which means at least my feet,
Will survive.

How We Sleep

I am given a plank of wood,
Together with four other women,
To sleep on.
Every time one person wants to move,
Everyone else needs to tag along.
Hup!
We yell.
Then we hoist ourselves on to our other side,
For a bit of relief.
That first night,
I sleep,
I don't know how.

My body must have,

Run out of steam.

All that loss.

My family.

My clothing.

My hair.

I sleep with,

My wooden clogs,

Under my head,

For a pillow,

And for safekeeping.

But at four in the morning,

When they wake us up,

My shoes are gone, too.

Tzel Appel

My first morning in Auschwitz,

I learn about the *Tzel Appel*.

Roll call, which happens at 4 a.m. each morning.

They stand us in rows of five,

Like rows of eggs

Waiting to be cracked open

And the German soldiers count.

Five.

Ten.

Fifteen.

Twenty.

Always a stick in their hands,

A snake,

Waiting to bite someone.

And if someone is missing,

Everyone suffers.

After roll call,

We get our food for the day.

Each one is given a small pot,

Which is filled with soup.

I am at the end of the line,

So my pot is nearly empty.

No family.

No shoes.

No food.

The world is a cracked egg.

And I, the bleeding yolk.

What Happened to the Others

We learn quickly,

What has happened to the others.

Those who could not work.

Old ones.

Young ones.

CHILDREN.

Sarah,

Chaim,

Danek.

Chocha.

Mula.

"You see those flames over there?"

They tell us.

"Those are your relatives."

Gassed.

Then incinerated,

Their souls smudging

The sky with ash.

Of course, nobody knows for sure.

And maybe my siblings,

My children,

Somehow,

Maybe,

Please,

Could they possibly still be—

No.

Lavatories

I used to have an indoor lavatory.

Pipes gurgling under my floors.

And after that, we had outdoor plumbing.

Clutching my skirts against me,

Making my way through the freezing night.

Then, we had an indoor bucket,

Tata emptying it every evening.

And now we have latrines.

Hundreds of people,

Loooooooooooong wooden planks,

With holes carved into them,

Trying desperately to keep our modesty

From melting into the pits below us.

Auschwitz August Weather Report

In the morning expect,

Boiling temperatures,

Unusual for this time of year.

The kind of weather that,

Makes your skin stick to,

Your blood.

And in the evenings,

Temperatures are expected to drop.

Every night.

Expect the cold,

To creep into your soul,

Like an unwanted visitor,

And expect it to stay until morning,

When the heat shoves it out,

And takes its place.

The Comb

In Auschwitz,

Somehow,

I am left with a treasure—

A mother-of-pearl comb.

This comb can have many uses.

I can use it to comb whatever hair I have.

I can trade it for bread.

Or,

I can simply hold onto it,

To remind myself that I am

A human being.

At *Tzel Appel* one morning,

A toothless woman catches sight of

My treasure.

"I propose a trade," she says.

"Give me your comb,

And I will give you my next bread."

A comb is wonderful,

But not as wonderful as

An extra bread—

An extra slice of life.

I give her the comb.

When she gets her next bread,

I approach her,

Like an innocent.

"Can I have the bread you promised me, please?"

"Go away!" she says.

"Or I will make you *kalt*."

I do not understand,

This way of talking.

"What does that mean,
That she will make me cold?"
I ask a woman standing nearby.
"A dead body is cold,"
The woman says.
"Don't ask her again.
I know her and
She will do as she says."
There is nothing fair
In Auschwitz.
And so,
I have no comb,
And
No bread.

Sick

There are a variety of
Ways to die,
In Auschwitz.
They can beat you to death,
For not standing straight,
During roll call.
They can shoot you,

For stepping out of line.

You can be selected,

For the gas chambers.

And sickness,

Is another way.

There are many sicknesses,

That plague people,

Who sleep so close to each other,

That breathe from the same air pockets,

Whose weeping sores,

Are left open and untreated.

When I wake up feeling,

Achy in every part of me,

And I can't tell,

Where my fever ends

And I begin,

I know there is trouble.

They take me to the *revier,*

This infirmary.

Ha!

More than two or three days there,

And they kill you.

In Ghetto Lodz,

The Germans tossed hospital patients,

Out of windows,

To their deaths—

For entertainment.

So the *revier* is not a place,

To recuperate in.

The doctor in the infirmary,

Is my dentist's wife!

Dr. Szapocznick!

She is as upset to see me here

As I am, to see her.

It is like looking in the mirror,

At what we used to be,

And what we have become.

She points to my face.

"You have a carbuncle," she says.

"It is a very bad infection on your face.

It is dripping into your blood.

There is no cure.

I'm so sorry,

But you will die."

I nod.

"I understand.

Please, though,
If you see my *tata*,
After I'm gone
Tell him—
Regarding my promise,
That I tried my best."

Electric Fences

The fences in Auschwitz,
Are electrified with,
Enough voltage,
To fry anyone,
Who touches them.
People toss themselves at
These fences
Like rubber balls,
A convenient choice.
There is nothing innocent about,
"I'll meet you at the fence."
One day,
I look longingly at that fence,
One quick shock,
And I can join my family,

Instead of waiting for this carbuncle
To do the job.
But.
That promise!
That blasted promise!

My Friend on the Train

After four weeks in Auschwitz,
They put us on a train.
Destination unknown.
I remember, when Danek was small,
I used to wonder what he thought,
Being schlepped from place to place,
With no say in the matter.
Now I am that baby,
Tugged and pulled,
Yanked and shoved,
Never knowing where my next stop is
And I am in less than loving hands.
But,
After four weeks of loneliness,
The girl next to me on the train,
Begins to speak with me.

"What's your name?" she asks me.

"I am Maniusia Adler."

"And I am Cipa Relkowitz," she says.

"From Warsaw."

"Oh! I have an aunt from there," I say.

"Do you know the Kober family?"

"I do!" Cipa says, her eyes dancing.

"And we are also chassidim."

A *landsman*!

When I hear these words,

I know that I will not be alone anymore.

Ripping Up a Death Sentence

I have a friend now,

But I still have a death sentence,

Sitting on my face,

Like a roosting pigeon.

This nasty carbuncle.

When we get on the train to Bergen-Belsen,

They give us a piece of bread,

And a small pat of margarine.

These delicacies are,

Inhaled by the starving passengers around me.

But I take that bit of fat,

And stick it to my carbuncle.

Then I tear an edge of my potato sack dress,

And bandage my wound.

When we arrive in Bergen-Belsen,

I take the bandage off,

And it lifts the entire carbuncle with it,

Ripping it from my face,

Prying death,

From my shoulders.

I have an empty hole in my cheek now,

The size of a small moon,

But I have traded my life for that hole,

And there is nothing empty about that.

Who Told Me?

Where did I get this idea?

To glue that margarine,

On to my wound,

Instead of gobbling it up?

How did I think,

To bandage it,

With the hem of my sack?

How did I cure myself,

Of a disease that the doctors,

Had no weapons to fight?

With no

Medicine,

Food,

Rest.

Tata would have said,

G-d planted the idea,

Like a seed in the dirt.

(I was certainly dirty enough.)

Tata would have said

That even in Auschwitz

The *Eibishter* in *Himmel*,

G-d in Heaven

Is stroking my cheek.

The thing is,

Even though:

Mama,

The children,

Ghetto Lodz,

Hungry,

Auschwitz,

Everything.

I know that Tata would have been right.

Bergen-Belsen

In Bergen-Belsen,

We roam like goats,

With no grass to nibble on.

At night,

We lay in tents, on a straw-covered floor.

To the right and the left of

Cipa and me,

Bodies fall,

In the morning sun,

And by the fragile light of

The night moon.

One night,

A cry wakes me.

Gevalt!

Someone lying close to me,

Thrashes once,

And then I hear that

Strange stillness of death,

I've grown accustomed to.

In the morning,

We stand to survey,

Whom the night has taken.

That noise I heard.

That scream.

I know that face.

It is the woman who

Stole my comb,

In Auschwitz.

It is her body that lies cold,

On the floor of Bergen-Belsen,

Der Eibishter hut ihr kalt gemacht.

G-d has made her cold.

All for a Pot

Rumors fly,

Like sparrows,

That we are moving.

Again.

"Gather yourselves!

We are leaving!"

We are leaving behind

All those dying,

From tuberculosis,

But Cipa and I,

Thank You, G-d,

Are moving on.

We gather for roll call in the morning,

And Cipa gasps.

"Maniusia! Our pots!"

In the camps,

There is only one thing more precious,

Than the skin on your back.

Your food pots.

I race back to our tent

To get my pot

And Cipa's.

But the Nazi

Head of the camp is there,

His whip flicking,

Like an angry snake.

That snake bites me,

Again and again

Ripping across my skin,

Like venom,

Until I collapse.

Two hours later,

I wake up,

Brush myself off,

Grab my pot, Cipa's pot,

And run to join the others.

Bergen-Belsen is not the sort of place

One wants to be left behind in.

Magdeburg

From Bergen-Belsen,

We arrive in Magdeburg.

Here, we are given

Prisoners' stripes to wear.

Warm clothing that

Covers from our scrawny necks,

Down to our knobby ankles.

Our pits and our scars,

Our welts and our pokey ribs.

I wouldn't be more excited,

If I'd been handed a wedding gown.

Ode to a Toothbrush

I don't even know

How I ended up with you,

But Mama would be so proud,

That even in the death camps,

I have you.

There is so very little food to clean,

From between my teeth,

And I expect my enamel,

Is dull as a camel's coat.

I share you,

Each morning and night,

With my friend Cipa,

Because what is mine,

Is hers, too.

But my dear toothbrush,

When I run your bristles,

Across my rows of tiny white windows,

I feel like I am shining me

Into a person.

Chosen for Work

As soon as we arrive in Magdeburg,

The heads of factories come,

In their clean white shirts,

To choose workers,

From among us.

Heaven forbid we should be bored!

But work is a word,

That means food ration,

Food ration is a word,

That means life.

And so like the orphaned children we are,

We pray for some factory owner,

To adopt us.

Cipa Relkowitz and I,

Pinch our cheeks hard,

Until strawberries blossom,

And we look a tad healthier,

Than half dead.

But so far,

Nobody has chosen,

Either of us.

Until Frauline Gertz.

Frauline Gertz chooses,

The sickest and most poorly among us,

Me with the crater face,

And eleven others,

With their own holes to speak of.

She tells us to follow her.

I am sorry that Cipa hadn't been chosen, too,

Until we arrive at our destination.

A room,

Filled with oversized cauldrons,

Leaking steam.

So this is the crematorium,

I think.

These monstrous vats are cooking,

Families.

Frauline Gertz is

A witch.

But Frauline Gertz tells us,

To peel potatoes

And when we lift those cauldron lids,

There is only soup inside.

Tangy,

Salty,

Delicious,

Soup.

"Eat, children," she whispers.

Not a crematorium.

A kitchen!

Not a witch.

A wonder!

Our job is,

To cook for the Germans,

But Frauline Gertz makes sure,

That we enjoy side benefits of the job,

Poking holes in,

Her own chances of living.

After so much tasting,

I don't need the food ration,

This work entitles me to.

The other eleven girls,

Bring their rations home,

For their mothers,

Sisters,

Cousins.

I have no mother,

Sister,

Cousin.

But I have Cipa Relkowitz,

And so each day,

I feed my friend.

Jewish?

Before the war,

When parks became off-limits for Jews,

The Adler children kept on playing.

Who knew we were Jews?

Our hair so light,

Our hearts so light.

Frauline Gertz watches me stir her pots.

She shakes her head as she passes me by.

"There is no way that you are truly Jewish,"

She says.

"It must be a mistake."

Thunder Rumbles

Every morning we wake at five,

For *Tzel Appel*,

And then I go to work,

For Frauline Gertz.

It is a long walk to the factory,

And a long walk back,

And all the way we hear rumbling,

Like drums.

"It's the Americans," girls say.

"They're already on the other side of

The Elbe River.

Soon they will be here,

To liberate us."

Soon the thunder rumbles grow closer.

And there are sirens.

Loud, yowling sirens.

Each time a siren sounds,

The Germans lock our barracks

And race to their shelters.

We can hear the buzz of the planes,

And when they let their bombs go,

The barracks shudder and groan,

But these are lullabies for us.

"Good," we say.

"Kill them all."

I am getting stronger,

From all my kitchen "work,"

And the Americans are coming.

Every day at Bergen-Belsen brings another morsel of

Hope.

Ten Officers

One morning,

At *Tzel Appel*,

There are ten German officers,

In spanking uniforms.

Each one has a snarling dog.

These officers have no fear,

In their eyes.

The smallest officer,

With a dog like a horse,

Announces to us,

"The Americans are on the other side

Of the Elbe River.

But you—all of you

Will not live to see them.

You are all leaving here today,"

They laugh.

"You have an appointment to be killed."

When we get to work,

The girls tell Frauline Gertz what he said.

"I will not let you die," she says.

"I will hide all of you."

The girls protest.

"But our mothers,
Sisters,
Cousins!"
"I will hide you with your
Mothers,
Sisters,
Cousins," she says.
"But my friend," I say.
Frauline Gertz shakes her head.
"I am so sorry, Maniusia.
But I cannot hide your friend.
She is not a relative.
And I need to draw a line somewhere."
I look at Frauline Gertz,
Whose fiancé has just been killed at war.
Kind Frauline Gertz,
Who is willing to hide us.
"I cannot abandon my friend," I say.
And so,
I return that day to be killed,
Along with Cipa Relkowitz.

The Walk of Death

"Sit down!"

The Germans yell at us,

As they march us out of Magdeburg,

Into a large clearing,

Where we sit,

Waiting.

"We will march all the way to Berlin!"

They scream.

Then they cock their weapons,

And they shoot,

Here,

There,

And everywhere.

We march on,

Leaving the dead and the injured,

Rotting in the field,

Me holding tight,

To the hand of my friend.

If you walk,

You live.

If your knees bend,

If you move out of line,

Just one centimeter,

If you cough,

Or slump,

Or your head looks wobbly,

You get a bullet,

And you never walk again.

All this walking,

On parched stomachs,

On stick legs,

On swollen feet,

With people falling all around you,

Like geese shot from the sky.

It is the walk of death.

Or the walk of life.

I wonder what it will be for me

And for Cipa.

Dead Horses

As we near Berlin,

The streets are pocked,

With dead horses.

Bloated and swollen,

And big as houses.

If you have never seen a dead horse,

Then you cannot imagine such a beast.

These dead horses,

Clog the thoroughfares.

We climb over these animals

With our raggedy limbs,

And it is like scaling,

The Alps.

PART 4

LIBERATION AND BEYOND
May 1945–December 1946

May 8, 1945

They bring us to a giant warehouse,

And close us inside.

And we wait.

Wait.

Wait.

Through the short windows,

We see a squat man,

Riding a chestnut horse.

He peeks around and

Seeing nothing of interest,

Leaves.

We wait.

Wait.

Wait.

Our officers of torture,

Who accompanied us,

All this way to Berlin,

Are nowhere.

Then more soldiers come.

And more.

But they are not German soldiers.

They are Russians.

They open the doors of our warehouse,

And they tell us,

That the war is over.

We

Are

Free.

What Freedom Feels Like

You imagine freedom will feel like,

One thousand birds,

Winging to the sun,

Air in your hair in the summer,

Stretching the sleep out of you in the morning,

Your favorite food piled from here to tomorrow,

A mountain of pillows,

But instead it feels like,

White.

Blankness.

Itchy scabs on your scalp.

Tired, achy feet,

Six years of memories,

Knocking the sense out of you,

With a tiny drip of hope,

That someone you love,

Might still walk the earth.

The Russians

The Russians,

Tell us we are free,

But they don't give us food,

To nourish our tiny bodies,

Or money,

To get out of this place.

They don't give medicines,

To the sick,

Who are falling like,

Trees in a vicious storm.

They don't give help,

To people who need more help than

Newly born babies.

They tell us we are free.

Free to do

WHAT?

Where To?

Even though,

They showed us the smoke in the camps,

Curling like a clenched fist in the sky,

Holding the ashes of our families,

We couldn't really believe it.

Not:

Sarah,

Chaim,

Danek.

And Tata,

He was young and strong,

And alive,

Oh, definitely alive.

But how to find them?

Mama always taught me,

If you ever get lost,

Don't go anywhere,

I'll find you

Where I left you.

That advice,

Is for a different kind of world.

There is one place Tata would surely go

To find me.

I am going home.

Walking

There are no automobiles,

Trains

Or trams,

To take me and Cipa home.

We have only our feet.

We walk,

And walk,

And walk.

There are so many of us walking,

The whole world is walking,

From country to country,

From war to peace,

From nothing to something.

Kilometers

If I could add up,

All the kilometers I've walked,

Throughout this war,

From city to city,

And country to country,

I'd come up with a number,

Too long to write.

Not to mention,

Many of those kilometers,

Were walked without,

Shoes.

The Russian Soldier

One important Russian soldier,

Walks alongside,

Cipa and me.

For hours and hours,

He won't leave our sides.

I can't imagine,

What he wants with us.

Until finally, at five in the morning,

He says,

"Are you Jewish?"

We do not look Jewish,

With our blond hair.

"Yes, we are."

He nods.

"I am Jewish, too!"

We share a

Jewish smile.

He reaches into his sack,

And gives us food for our journey.

"Where are you going?" he asks us.

"To Poland," we say.

"To find our families."

He shakes his head slowly,

His mouth a grim line.

"There is no family," he says.

"They killed everyone."

Ribbons

Throngs of people walk,

Everyone identified,

By their ribbons.

We wear yellow ribbons,

Instead of yellow stars.

Poles wear green ribbons.

Russians, red.

It might have looked like,

A parade,

If not for the sunken faces,

And no waving,

Or smiling.
At one point Cipa says,
"Maniusia, I don't know,
If it is smart to tell the world,
That we are Jewish.
Not yet."
And so our ribbons,
Go fluttering away,
Like spiders on a breeze.

Poznań

We arrive in Poznań, Poland,
Where a train idles,
Ready to take us,
To Lodz.
A train!
It is a train meant,
For animals,
But there is nobody as unspoiled as
Me.
But—
I look at Cipa.
"I cannot get on this train," I say.

"Today is Shabbos.

Travel is not allowed."

I have promised Tata

To always remember who I am

And who I am

Would never desecrate the holy Shabbos.

The conductor hears me.

"If you do not get on this train,

There will not be another,

For a whole month."

If I stay in Poznań,

I could starve,

Or worse.

And I know that,

Travel is allowed on Shabbos,

In order to save a life.

Besides, it is not as if

I will be driving the train myself,

So I issue my own

Rabbinic ruling,

And allow myself,

To board the train.

Rabbi Maniusia Adler!

Liberation and Beyond

Return to Lodz

We arrive in Lodz,

Cipa and me.

And we walk to S'ro'dmiejska 32,

Where the Bais Yaakov school used to be.

Where my great-uncle, Shmiel Zonabend, used to be principal,

Which has now become a *gmina*,

A place to find yourself,

The center for Jewish—everything.

This great institution,

Where girls learned Torah.

I see this place,

And my stomach feels wobbly,

At the thought of what was,

And what has happened.

These halls,

With pitchers-ful of girls

Spilling down the stairs,

Hold no students anymore.

Those students,

Are now spindly bones,

Their smiles,

Turned to ash,

In a fiery sky.

Paula Waiskol

At the *gmina*,

Cipa and I can read lists of names

And notes from people

Looking for people,

We pray to find,

Some sign of life,

From our families.

The first person that I see at the *gmina*

Is Paula Waiskol,

A neighbor from,

My previous life,

In Pabianice.

"Maniusia!" she says,

Embracing my tired, skinny self.

I nearly cry,

But I know if I open myself to tears,

I might flood the city.

"Have you seen my father?" I ask her.

She shakes her head a sad, slow shake.

"You must come and live with us!" she says.

"You can't be out on the streets.

It's dangerous!"

Oh, how I long for:

A warm bed,

Warm food,

Warm words.

"That would be wonderful," I say.

I look across the room at Cipa,

Who is reading a list,

Her tongue poking,

From the corner of her mouth.

"My friend, Cipa Relkowitz,

If I am the right arm,

She is the left.

Can you take her in, too?"

Paula shakes her head,

A sad, slow shake.

"I'm terribly sorry.

I barely have one extra bed,

And feeding one extra mouth,

Was already going to be,

A brick on my head."

I straighten myself up.

"Well, then,

I thank you anyway.

We will be fine."

Yes.

Me and Cipa.

Will be

Fine?

A Place to Stay

Nights,

We sleep in the hallway of a place

For girls like us.

Girls who have nobody to speak for them.

Nobody to invite them in.

We are nobodies,

Who know nobody.

That's a lot of nobody.

At least I have Cipa

And Cipa has me,

Together we are,

A little bit of

Somebody.

Cipa

A few days later,

Cipa and I are doing,

What we always do,

Scouring the world,

For mothers,

Brothers,

Others.

When I hear Cipa yell,

"Feter Shloime!"

Like a ghost,

Cipa's uncle has appeared,

And all of a sudden,

She is really,

Somebody.

"I'm so happy I found you," he says.

"I thought there was nobody left.

You will come and live with me."

Cipa looks at me.

She shrugs.

I shrug.

He will have too many mouths to feed,

To take me on.

Cipa and I will find a home together,

With time.

But she looks at me,

And I can already see,

The leaving,

In her eyes.

"This is my chance," she says.

"I am going with him."

And Cipa Relkowitz,

Leaves with her uncle,

Me, waving goodbye.

A Bitter Taste

As I sleep that night,

I can't help the taste of lemon,

Lodged in my throat,

Thinking of how twice,

I lay across the butcher's board,

For Cipa,

When all along,

She had no intention,

Of doing it for me.

Pabianice

I am like a pitted fruit,

Without anyone,

Not even Cipa,

Who I thought was—

Well…so I thought.

I walk the streets of Lodz,

And the Jews call out "*amcha*" one to another,

I am of your nation.

And you are of mine.

It helps,

But it is not enough.

I think to travel to Pabianice.

Maybe there, I will find some signs of my family.

I take the tram, forty-five minutes, and I am in the city of my birth.

There, I meet a lawyer who is helping the Jews.

"You must go to city hall," he tells me.

"Make a claim on your house!"

I look at him, his eyes like black beetles, eyes that don't understand.

"I have no Tata, no Mama, no sisters or brothers.

With what would I fill a house?"

I do not go to city hall.

Where Have All the Adlers Gone?

The streets in Pabianice,

Are so familiar,

The air feels,

Like an old jacket.

But this place that was once

Dripping with Adlers,

Has run dry.

The only Adler that I can find in Pabianice,

Is me.

Signs of Life

At the *gmina* in Pabianice,

Someone tells me,

"There is a postcard addressed to your uncle here!"

My heart thumps like a kicking, screaming child against my ribs

And I find it!

A postcard addressed to—

Feter Yankel,

Whose voice was lost,

In a prison in Lodz.

Just seeing his name,

Feels like a kiss.

It is a postcard sent,

From my *tata's* brother,

Uncle Beirish.

It says,

My wife and my two children

Are alive,

Bracha and Leibel.

Our daughter Zisel, her husband and baby—

We don't know.

I look forward to seeing who is alive.

I clutch that postcard to my chest,

And it feels like a hug.

I knew it.

Cousin Leibel made footprints,

Even in Siberia.

More Good News

As I stand,

With this letter dancing in my mind,

A woman approaches me.

"Maniusia?" she asks.

I search her face,

But do not see anything familiar about it.

"Your father is Yitzchak Adler!"

My heart leaps.

"Do you know where he is?"

She shakes her head.

"I'm sorry. No.

But I am his second cousin.

Helcia Horowitz.

I survived with one son.

The others are gone.

We are staying in Lodz now.

Do you have somewhere to stay?

Or are you alone?"

Am I alone?

I cannot imagine,

That there is anyone on earth,

More alone than me.

I have no Mama,

Tata,

Chaim,

Sarah,

Danek,

Baby,

Cipa Relkowitz.

I have a postcard from Russia,

But no way of getting there.

"Thank you. That would be—

Everything."

Goodbye, Pabianice

I hug the stones,

With the curl of my body,

Under familiar stars,

Freckling the sky.

Surrounded by the breath,

Of my family,

I say goodbye

To my Pabianice.

Saved by Accident

With no other choice,

I go back to Lodz,

That city which robbed me

Of years in my life

Which were supposed to be

Important.

The war is over but,

People are still busy

Hating Jews,

Hurting Jews.

I am not safe.

As I walk the streets,

Searching for signs of life,

A man shoves me,

Into the lobby of a building,

Rough against,

The wall.

"Get in!" he shouts.

"They're killing Jews out there!"

A few of us huddle there,

My savior

A man

And some others,

While a few shots sound outside.

I look around the lobby.

They are all blond,

Like me.

I realize that my savior

Thinks me a gentile.

If not for that fact—

I could have survived:

Ghetto Lodz,

Auschwitz,

Bergen-Belsen,

Magdeburg,

And the March of Death,

Just to have it end here.

Sewing

In Lodz I get a job,

Sewing the collars of men's shirts,

To earn a few *groszy*,

To live.

And I wait,

I'm not sure for what.

One day, I get a letter from

An old friend.

Maniusia,

Your Tata is alive.

Come to Germany,

To the Displaced Persons Camp,

Foehrenwald.

Someone there will

Know where he is.

With love,

Dziunia Baumgarten.

Tata?

Tata?

Do you hear me?

I am alive, too!

Germany

How can I,

Who has no passport,

No identification at all,

No family,

No money,

Nothing,

Get to Foehrenwald,

To find that someone,

Who knows that something,

About my Tata?

Once again,

Rumors are flying

In Lodz.

There are smugglers,

And Dziunia gave me the names of two others,

Trying to make their way to Germany.

Somehow,

I will make my way to my—

Tata.

Yom Kippur

The train to Germany

Travels like this.

Stand two days.

Travel two hours.

Stand one day.

Travel one hour.

This train needs

A lot of sleep.

One of those standing days,

Is Yom Kippur,

The holiest day of

The Jewish year.

On this day,

You cannot eat,

Or drink.

In the camps,

Fasting was no different

From any other day of the year.

But now,

It is my choice.

When the water is passed

Around the hot, metal car

And I refuse,

Time and time again,

People ask me why.

"It's Yom Kippur," I say.

They can't believe,

That someone still believes.

They can't imagine,

That after all we've been through,

Someone will still give up

Anything

For G-d.

"I won't eat," I say.

The rest of my words,

Stick in my throat.

What can I say?

I don't know why I can't,

Pass a morsel of food,

Through my lips.

Maybe it is my promise.

"Do not forget who you are."

And maybe it is something

Inside of me,

That makes my faith,

Cling to me like a burr.

I do know that,

I will never abandon G-d,

Because then,

I would be truly

Alone.

Caught

This train,

Which stops and starts,

Like an irritating cough,

Every time it moves,

You feel your spirits lift,

And every time it stalls,

You want to pull your hair out.

But finally,

We reach the German border.

They check our papers,

Which are not in order.

There is nothing

Orderly about us.

They turn our rickety train around.

And send us back to Poland.

Again

Nothing will keep me,

From finding Tata.

And so I try again.

And this time,

We make it through,

To Germany.

When I come to Foehrenwald,

It is already night.

The moon is full,

And round as a pie.

I am looking for someone,

Who knows something,

About someone,

That I love more,

Than the shoes on my feet,

And that is saying quite a lot.

When I hear the sound

Of Torah learning,

That soft chant,

It makes the hairs on my arms,

Dance.

I know that whoever learns the holy Torah,

Will also know where Tata is.

I follow that sound,

Like a charmed snake,

Till I come to a set of stairs,

With peeling paint,

And planks missing,

Like pulled teeth.

Climb those stairs,

Open the door

And a shaft of light falls on me,

Lights me up.

Two men sit there,

The Talmud open between them,

And a third man nearby.

"Who are you?" they ask me.

"I am Maniusia Adler.

I am looking for word of my father.

Yitzchak Adler."

They shake their heads.

"So sorry.

We don't know him."

I close my eyes,

Feel them burning,

Pictures of Tata flicker behind my closed lids.

"Wait!" the man who was not learning says.

"Adler. Do you know Reb Beirish Adler?"

My eyes flit open.

"That's my uncle."

The man jumps up, excited.

"I spoke to him just yesterday!

In Paris!

He and his family came back from Russia.

And I remember now that he was looking for you.

When I speak with him again,

I will tell him that I saw you.

My name is Leibish Spero."

I scrawl a quick note,

To give to my uncle,

Wondering if it will actually arrive by him.

Then I turn to leave,

But a question runs itself,

Up the rim of my tongue,

Tickling.

"Tell me," I say quickly.

"My Cousin Leibel—

Is he a big rabbi,

Or a famous scientist?"

Mr. Spero laughs.

"He is neither of those.

Yet.

But he learned in Yeshivas Chachmei Lublin.

Where you need to memorize

Two hundred *blatt* of the Talmud,

Just to get in.

That boy is very smart."

I leave that room,

Feeling lighter and heavier

All at the same time.

No Tata

Weeks in Foehrenwald,

Don't bring me any closer,

To finding Tata.

But I hear that I have an aunt,

Chocha Ruchka,

In Bergen-Belsen,

With her daughters Tema, Sala, and Rivtcha,

And so I return,

To Bergen-Belsen.

My aunt and my cousins,

Hold me close,

And treat me like the family I am.

I spend the holiday of Sukkos,

In Bergen-Belsen

A place as familiar as

A repeating nightmare.

I keep my search for Tata up,

And I'm fed one morsel of information,

By two men, Leibel Eisner and Aaron Rosenbloom.

"Maniusia," they say.

"Of course we remember your father.

This past Pesach in Buchenwald,

Only one month before liberation,

He saved up all of his potato peels,

Instead of eating them himself,

And he gave them out to the other Jews

So that they would not give up

And eat leavened bread during Pesach, Passover,

As commanded by G-d."

And so I know that,

One month before liberation,

Tata was alive,

Being—

Tata.

But

Of course Tata would think of his beloved G-d,

In Buchenwald.

I will never forget how,

Minutes after losing his children,

He found me,

And made me promise,

A promise that made me and G-d above,

Forever friends.

But,

I have a realization,

Here in Bergen-Belsen.

That tears at my gut,

And makes me vomit.

My realization:

Just as there is nothing that can stand

Between me and finding my *tata*,

There is nothing that would stand,

Between my *tata* and his finding me.

This knowledge lands between my eyes,

Like a bullet.

And I know then,

That Tata is gone,

Joined with the One he loved,

Most of all.

Moishele Hirschman

Bergen-Belsen,

Is the world's worst hotel,

And despite my darling aunt

And cousins,

I long to leave.

I know where I want to—

Well,

I know *who* I want to get to.

Cousin Leibel.

Though I have no idea how to do that.

Moishele Hirschman appears,

Just when I itch to run,

He is from Pabianice,

He is a cousin

Who used to work for Tata

And he knows Warszawska Street,

Where every house was an Adler.

"There's nothing doing," he says.

"You are coming back to Munich with me.

I live there with a friend,

His brother,

Two sisters.

No matter.

You will come."

I do not have

A line full of offers,

So I go to Munich.

Munich

I stay in Munich,

From Sukkos in the fall,

Through Pesach in the spring.

Until,

Moishele Hirschman is out one day,

And he hears people talking about a soldier—

From America!

Who is here in Germany looking for lost children.

Moishele Hirschman is a *yenta*,

With his nose *shmecking* into everything,

He runs to hear more.

The American soldier is Rabbi Isaac Levine.

He is a part of the *Vaad L'hatzolas Hanoar*,

An organization helping to save lost children—

Like me.

"What's going on?" Moishele asks,

Pushing through the crowd.

"I am looking for a young girl," Rabbi Levine says.

"Her uncle is the head of *Vaad L'hatzolas Hanoar* in Paris.

I have her photo."

"Well, then! Let me see it!" Moishele says.

You've probably already guessed.

The photo is of a girl—

Me.

But How to Get There?

Feter Beirish,

Wants me to come to Paris,

To be his—

His—

Child!

He heads the *Vaad L'hatzolas Hanoar*,

That saves children

All the time.

He will know how

To bring me to Paris.

Right?

A World Away

But.

He tries getting me there,

By plane,

And that falls through.

By train.

But guess what?

We are caught at the border,

And sent back to Munich.

My life has become,

A series of repeating problems.

Finally

Feter Beirish gets me a visa,

To Santa Domingo,

With a transit to France.

Santa Domingo.

The words roll on my tongue,

Like sweet grapes.

I pack my torn valise,

With my shabby things,

And I thank my dear hosts.

I leave knowing,

That I am finally headed,

Toward a new life,

Or at least,

That possibility.

Paris

I ride to Paris,

On a military train,

Made for elegant ladies.

And I look like,

A lump.

With a holey valise.

And mismatched clothing.

When I arrive in Paris,

I don't know which way to turn,

To get to 258 Saint-Martin Street.

A kind Parisian lady,

Offers to bring me there.

She gives me money for a taxi

And I take her address,

So that I can return it,

When I am a person again.

And all of a sudden,

I am there.

The lobby of the building,

Has a concierge.

"Which floor?" he asks,

Looking at me like

I am a wet newspaper,

Blown in by a storm.

I do not know which floor.

I throw my shoulders back,

And try to look at ease.

"The Adler family, please."

"Third floor," he tells me.

The entire third floor apartment,

Belongs to the Adlers.

The main entrance is for,

Avraham and Manya Adler,

Cousins.

Feter Beirish and Chocha Raizel,

Live where the help used to stay.

I knock on the main door,

And my cousins Avraham and Manya answer.

"Maniusia!" Manya cries,

Hugging me,

And then kissing me.

But I do not know that in Paris,

You kiss on both cheeks,

So we get all tangled,

In a kissy mess.

These cousins are dressed

So fine.

One can tell that they are not

Leftovers from the camps.

Like me.

Home

"Let me call Beirish and Raizel!"

Cousin Manya cries,

Her voice is big,

Her hands move like butterflies.

And then, there they are,

My *feter* and *chocha*,

Gerrer chassidim, just like Tata,

With his long beard,

And his curled *peyos*,

And already it feels like,

Home.

Catching Up

How can you contain,

Six years like the ones I lived,

Into one conversation?

Into one story?

Into one anything?

I try to start at the beginning,

Try hurrying through the ugly middle,

I still don't know where it will end,

So that part is easy.

One Hundred Years

All through the night,

We cry

And laugh.

I don't know where the laughing comes from,

But it feels sweet.

Chocha Raizel tells me that,

They lost their:

Daughter,

Son-in-law,

Granddaughter,

And another unborn child,

That she was growing.

Feter Beirish tells me,

"You are smarter than most,

Because at seventeen years,

You've seen more than people,

Who lived one hundred of them."

Feter Beirish

Feter Beirish

Is so very different from Tata,

But he is his brother,

The same blood runs through them,

The same blood that runs through me.

I feel like we are all part

Of the same river

And finally,

Instead of feeling like I am standing still,

I begin to flow.

The Story My Clothing Doesn't Tell

I come to Paris,

Wearing a small sweater with

A prisoner's cross on the back,

And in my scruffy valise,

I've held onto my stripes.

My cheeks pink as,

Chocha Raizel,

Empties my bags.

"I am proud to have you,

In my home,"

Chocha Raizel says,

As she tosses my clothing,

Into dark bags,

Meant for disposal.

"You have nothing to be ashamed of.

I know from your clothing,

That nobody provided for you,

That you didn't run around like

A *vilde chayah*!"

Because of my threadbare valise,

Chocha Raizel knows that I kept to myself

And held on

To my father's ways.

That promise!

Is going to become very important,

Very soon.

Cousin Leibel

"Hello, Maniusia,"

Cousin Leibel need only say that

And I am sold.

Cousin Leibel and I,

Get along like rubbed sticks,

We become the best of friends,

Again.

Like the past six years,

Hasn't wedged between us.

He is still a troublemaker,

In his own grown-up way,

And the spark in me that I've lost,

Somewhere in Pabianice,

Finds its way back

To being lit,

In his company.

But he went to school,

Even in Siberia.

He knows the world,

Like the palm of his hand,

While my brain is only stuffed

With Ghetto and Camps and Death.

If he is a thumb,

I am the tip of a pinky,

I don't like feeling small,

Next to Cousin Leibel.

Cousin Bracha, Too

Cousin Bracha is

Smart in her own right.

I like being,

In her company.

But she is already promised,

To the great-grandson of the Rebbe of Gur!

Such *mechubadik yichus*!

He is in Israel,

Waiting to marry her,

And while she waits,

She needs to behave,

Proper and *mechubadik*.

So I still prefer,

Cousin Leibel.

Nothing Special

My family is

Always with me.

Tata

And Mama

And the children.

Like open sores,

All over my body.

If this were my pain alone,

I think I would simply crumple up

And disappear.

But our Sages say,

Tzaras rabim chatzi nechamah,

A pain that befalls many,

Is half a consolation.

The streets of Europe are

Pocked with Jews,

Missing pieces of themselves—

Mothers, fathers, brothers, others.

I am nothing special.

Just as the others move forward,

So will I.

Shabbos

As holy as Shabbos is,

The long summer afternoons,

Where one can't do much,

Of anything,

Press on me,

And even more so on

Cousin Leibel.

We walk the streets of Paris,

To pass the hours,

Until the stars twinkle down,

From a navy blue sky,

And we can recite the Havdalah to end Shabbos.

We talk of

Family,

Life,

Religion,

And eventually,

Marriage.

Pinkies and Thumbs

Even though Cousin Leibel,

Would have preferred to marry a dark-haired girl

And I am blond

He likes what he sees,

Inside of me.

And at times like these,

People tend to look

A little bit deeper.

Feter Beirish and Chocha Raizel,

Know that I have made a promise to Tata

And for that promise, I am worthy of their son.

They trust me to hold the reins,

Keeping Leibel on the straight and narrow path

Of our forefathers.

And so in some ways,

I am the thumb

And Leibel is the pinky tip.

This feels more fair.

Us First

Chassidim do not make important decisions

Without the blessing of the Grand Rabbi.

Feter Beirish asks the Rebbe of Gur,

The great Imrei Emes,

Whether Leibel and I are a suitable match.

"This match has my blessing,"

The Rebbe says.

The custom is that

The oldest child marries first.

That means we must marry before Bracha.

And so it happens that,

I am officially,

Starting over.

My Wedding

The day before my wedding,

I lie in bed,

From sunrise to sunset,

And I cry until I'm limp.

Feter Beirish and Chocha Raizel try so hard,

But nothing can disguise the fact that,

Chocha Raizel is not Mama

And Feter Beirish is definitely not—

Tata.

My Wedding Day

I borrow a wedding dress,

And a veil,

I look like the clouds.

On the way to the synagogue for the ceremony,

The driver says,

"In France you don't give compliments unless it's the truth.

Otherwise, it's best to say nothing at all."

He nods.

"You are a very beautiful bride."

I say nothing, but—

I remember a beauty contest back in Pabianice.

I was the winner.

If what he says is true,

It is hard to believe

There is something from before the war

That I have not lost.

More Family

My married name will still be Adler,

Which means I will always have a piece of Tata in me,

To carry on,

And I still have a piece of myself,

Too.

But more than that,

Cousin Leibel

Is also Husband Leibel.

And Chocha Raizel,

Is my mother-in-law.

Feter Beirish,

Is my father-in-law,

And Cousin Bracha,

My sister-in-law.

My dear Tata,

Who should rest in peace,

Was not only my cousin's uncle,

He was my husband's father-in-law.

And so on.

By marrying Cousin Leibel,

I'm creating so many relatives

From the few I have left.

Seven Circles

The *chazzan* sings,

And all around me,

Guests cry,

For the orphan bride.

As I walk seven circles around my groom,

Under a white awning,

I look up at the blank white canopy,

And I feel white and

So very empty,

Because of all who are missing,

But I look at my aunt and uncle,

And then at my Leibel,

His twinkly blue eyes,

Making a blessing and

Sipping from a silver wine goblet,

And I feel so very full.

I have come so far from—

That little girl who needed her governess

To usher her through her day,

And now—

As a light breeze blows the veil in front of my eyes—

I think of the weddings that will never be

But I also think of the wedding that is happening now.

I lift my eyes

And I thank the Lord that I am still here.

Beginning again—

Like a fresh skein of wool.

Making something out of nothing

Stretching my promise

To create a new family

To create eternity.

Author's Postscript

After marrying my grandfather, my grandmother, Miriam (Maniusia) Adler, made *aliyah* to Israel with her husband and her in-laws, who were also her aunt and uncle. Safta traveled on her sister-in-law Bracha's visa, since Bracha had already moved to Israel earlier to marry the great-grandson of the Sfas Emes, a famous rabbi from Gur. When Safta and her family disembarked from the ship that brought them to Israel, they took a taxi ride to Tel Aviv, and they were shot at by Arabs along the way. It was a rude welcome—and things in Israel did not get much easier.

Then, in 1948, the War of Independence made things even more difficult. There was a siege on Jerusalem, and therefore food was scarce. Their apartment was in the line of fire. At one point, a Jordanian shell crashed near the window of their apartment, and shrapnel landed in my Aunt Naomi's crib while they were out. A grenade also landed at the foot of their beds and made a hole in the floor when they weren't home. Eventually, they left to America.

My Safta and Saba lived in Queens, New York until Saba, my grandfather, passed away in May of 1995. Saba was a multi-talented, brilliant man and an exquisitely talented artist. His paintings depicting the Holocaust and pre-war European Jewry have been featured in exhibitions. He also had a beautiful voice, and people still remember how he sang so beautifully when he *davened* for the *amud*. He received his humble beginnings on the streets of Pabianice, with my Safta holding his hat for donations.

Saba and Safta had four children together. Today, their descendants number tens of grandchildren and great-grandchildren.

After Safta was widowed, she remarried a most wonderful, special man, our Zeidy Mark.

A few years ago, Safta was perusing the newspaper when she saw that an insurance company called *Asecuratzioni Generali* was offering compensation to anyone who had purchased a plan from them in pre-war Europe. The name immediately jarred my grandmother's memory as something that had been written on one of the papers her dear Tata had entrusted her with on the train ride to Auschwitz. Though she had to leave everything on the train, whatever she had seen in that sheaf of papers remained indelible in her mind. The company was astounded that she'd remembered, considering how young she'd been. She was able to cash in on the insurance policy her Tata had taken out in her name.

After the war, Safta and Cipa became reacquainted, and they are still friends to this day. Safta told me that it is difficult to pass judgment during times of war, and so Cipa was forgiven.

Today Safta still lives in New York. She has been invited to lecture numerous times in both the United States and Israel about her experiences during the war. Audiences are always incredibly moved by her story and her delivery. She is a devoted mother, grandmother, and great-grandmother who is loved and cherished by all of us.

I had always been curious about my Safta's story, but growing up she was not ready to share her story with anyone at all. I recall all of the *yahrtzeit* candles she used to light every Yom Kippur when we went to sleep at her house, and how she cried during *Ne'ilah* in a way that was different than the cries of someone who hasn't experienced the loss of everything and everyone she loved. But I didn't understand.

Later, Safta began to open up, but I was already busy with my own life, getting married and building a family; it didn't occur to me to sit down and get her story. About a year ago, my cousin, Tamar Fineberg, asked her mother, Leora, if someone could write up Safta's story. She attended Yavneh Academy, where a Holocaust-based play was put on by the eighth graders every year. She wanted her eighth grade year to feature her own Safta's story. The problem was that the play was written by the students, under the direction of a skilled playwright, using a manuscript or a book as the basis for the play. Without a book about Safta's life, there could be no play.

My Aunt Leora reached out to me, the family writer, to see if I might be interested in taking on this project. To be honest, I was very nervous. First of all, I'm a busy mother of a large family, and I write full-time for a living. I couldn't imagine where I would fit this into my schedule. Secondly, I was afraid to open up my Safta's memory box. She has an impeccable memory, and I knew how difficult it would be for her to dredge up all of the painful experiences she had gone through. Finally, there was the issue of geography, as I live in Israel and she in America.

After thinking it through carefully, I decided that I wanted to go ahead with it. I wanted to get Safta's story down as a legacy for our family, and in order to honor the memories of my relatives who had perished. My Aunt Leora helped set Safta and me up via Skype, and we began the process of interviewing.

At first there were technical glitches. My grandmother is a diminutive woman, and there were times I could only see the top of her head while I was speaking with her. Though these kinks were ironed out by Leora and some of her technically savvy children, there were other issues that cropped up. For example, when your Safta tells you about losing her parents and her siblings, through a barrage of tears, and you can't even reach out to hug her, it feels cruel. I was grateful and amazed when Safta traveled to Israel on her own, and we were able to complete the process together, in person. These are memories I will cherish forever.

Interviewing Safta also acquainted me with relatives I never had the chance to know. Our son Yitzchak is named after Safta's father *Hy"d*, and our son Yaakov is named after Feter Yankel *Hy"d*, who is also mentioned in this book. I am grateful that my children will have a book in which to read about their illustrious namesakes.

This work is deeply personal, yet it is also based upon historical events. The book was culled almost entirely from Safta's impeccable memories. Her memory is so unusual she was able to remember the exact spellings of street names from the ghetto, more than seventy years later. I did, however, feel the need to acquaint myself with her surroundings through my own research as well. In this vein, I researched the Lodz ghetto through books, photos, and documentaries. I had also visited Poland and the concentration camps myself, which helped to give me a better picture. All those things notwithstanding, I apologize for any historical errors and accept them as my own.

To contact or to schedule a speaking engagement with the author and/or Miriam (Maniusia) Adler, please write to: authorvisits101@gmail.com.

Maniusia and her brother Chaim.

Maniusia's family's home, Warszawska 37.

Maniusia's tenth birthday party; children are dressed up for a show. Maniusia is standing in the middle of the back row, wearing a hat. The child on the right, in the second row from the front, is Sarah. The boy wearing glasses is Chaim, and the baby being held in the back row is Fishel Dan.

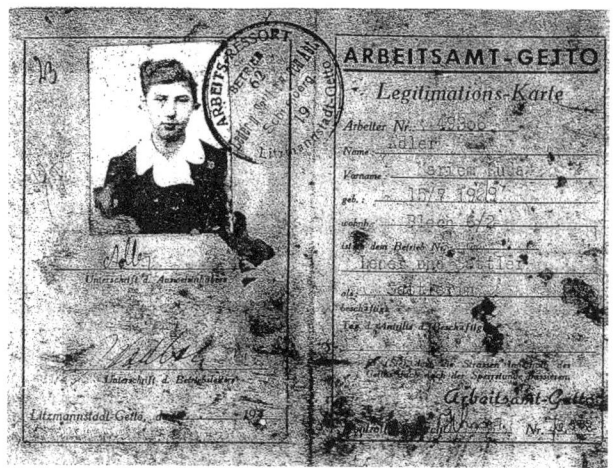
Copy of Maniusia's work papers from the Lodz ghetto.

Maniusia's father, Reb Yitzchak Adler (front right side).

Wedding picture of Leibel Adler.

Maniusia's mother, Chana Zisel Adler, at a cousin's wedding; she is standing to the left of the bride, Miriam Sara (Mandel) Dunkelman. To the right is Aunt Balcha, Feter Yankel's wife.

Wedding picture of Maniusia (Miriam) Adler.

Paintings of Ari (a.k.a "Cousin Leibel," Yehuda Aryeh Leib) Adler. Though his paintings were of professional quality, they were extremely personal to him and he only reluctantly agreed to sell a handful of them for profit.

About the Author

Yael Mermelstein's stories and essays have appeared in numerous publications and this is her tenth published book. Her stories have been approved by the Israeli Ministry of Education for study for the English matriculation exams in Israel and they have been published in nationwide textbooks. Yael's children's book, *Izzy the Whiz and Passover McClean*, was a P.J. library selection, distributed to children country-wide. She is the recipient of the Sydney Taylor Manuscript Award. Yael lives in Israel with her family and her pet computer.